PRAYER CHANGES THINGS

Prayer Secrets

Dag Heward-Mills

Parchment House

PRAYER CHANGES THINGS
PRAYER SECRETS

Copyright © 2023 Dag Heward-Mills

First published 2023 by Parchment House

Find out more about Dag Heward-Mills at:

Healing Jesus Campaign
Email: evangelist@daghewardmills.org
Website: www.daghewardmills.org
Facebook: Dag Heward-Mills
Twitter: @EvangelistDag

ISBN : 978-1-64330-612-4

Contents

CHAPTER 1

Prayer Changes Things

Be careful for nothing; but in every thing by prayer and supplication with thanksgiving let your requests be made known unto God.

Philippians 4:6

Achange is coming through prayer! God is moving in your life! His angels are ready to be deployed to intervene in your crises. Whatever is a source of concern to you will be addressed by prayer. Prayer does have an effect on our lives! Prayer changes things! You may not have money but you can pray! You may not know any important person but you can pray! Prayer changes things!

Through these few pages, your prayer life will move to the highest level it has ever been. Your family is going to be amazed at how prayerful you have become. Prayer changes things! Don't wait until you have a crisis before you pray. Learn how to pray now! It is more important to know how to pray than to have a degree at the university.

1. **Prayer changes things: Prayer changes your countenance!**

> And it came to pass about an eight days after these sayings, he took Peter and John and James, and went up into a mountain to pray. AND AS HE PRAYED, THE FASHION OF HIS COUNTENANCE WAS ALTERED, and his raiment was white and glistering. And, behold, there talked with him two men, which were Moses and Elias: who appeared in glory, and spake of his decease which he should accomplish at Jerusalem. But Peter and they that were with him were heavy with sleep: and when they were awake, they saw his glory, and the two men that stood with him.
>
> Luke 9:28-32

Through prayer appearance will change! Through prayer, a great change will come into your life. Your countenance will change. People will see the glory of God on your life. A great change takes place whenever you pray. Instead of shame people will see glory. Expect a great change indeed!

As Jesus prayed, His very appearance changed. Prayerful people are more attractive than prayerless people. You will become more handsome as you spend time praying. Somebody will find you sweet, appealing and comely when you pray. There will be a change.

Expect a great change to start in your life from the moment you start praying. Whatever could not change before you started praying will start changing after you pray. The change that took place on Jesus' countenance was supernatural. The change that will take place on your countenance will be supernatural.

You were not able to get a beloved by changing of hairstyles and putting on of makeup. The real change will not come from makeup or Brazilian wigs. The real change will come through prayer. Expect to become attractive, appealing, nice and good-looking as you go deeper into prayer.

2.   Prayer changes things: Prayer brings dead things back to life!

Jesus said, Take ye away the stone. Martha, the sister of him that was dead, saith unto him, Lord, by this time he stinketh: for he hath been dead four days. Jesus saith unto her, Said I not unto thee, that, if thou wouldest believe, thou shouldest see the glory of God? THEN THEY TOOK AWAY THE STONE FROM THE PLACE WHERE THE DEAD WAS LAID. And JESUS LIFTED UP HIS EYES, AND SAID, FATHER, I THANK THEE THAT THOU HAST HEARD ME. And I knew that thou hearest me always: but because of the people which stand by I said it, that they may believe that thou hast sent me.

John 11:39-42

Through prayer, bad news will become good news! The stinking smell of your condition will be removed and replaced through prayer. Prayer changes the stink on you.

3

Prayer can change the worst evil in your life. What is the worst thing that has happened in your life? Prayer can make a difference! Prayer can make a change! Remember that prayer changes things!

When Jesus encountered the dead body of Lazarus, He prayed a short prayer. His short prayer changed everything.

Lazarus' stinking body was changed into a living normal body.

Even your short prayer can change everything in your life.

Expect a great change to come as you pray.

Do not sit down and make philosophical quotations from Socrates and other wise men.

Start praying right now! Prayer changes things! There are many things that cannot be changed in the natural. Only prayer can change them. Believe in prayer! Believe that God can change everything through prayer. Prayer changes things!

3.   **Prayer changes things: Prayer changes the date that you leave this world!**

AND WHEN ELISHA WAS COME INTO THE HOUSE, BEHOLD, THE CHILD WAS DEAD, AND LAID UPON HIS BED. HE WENT IN THEREFORE, AND SHUT THE DOOR UPON THEM TWAIN, AND PRAYED UNTO THE LORD. And he went up, and lay upon the child, and put his mouth upon his mouth, and his eyes upon his eyes, and his hands upon his hands: and he stretched himself upon the child; and the flesh of the child waxed warm. Then he returned, and walked in the house to and fro; and went up, and stretched himself upon him: and the child sneezed seven times, and the child opened his eyes.

2 Kings 4:32-35

When Elijah came into the house and found a dead child he decided to pray. Prayer changes things! Through prayer, the young man was raised from the dead.

He no longer had to die as a young person.

His date for leaving this world was changed.

His years were prolonged by prayer.

Years were added unto him through prayer.

Prayer changed many things.

Prayer will change your life.

Prayer will change the lives of those you pray for.

4.   Prayer changes things: Prayer changes the number of years that you live!

In those days was Hezekiah sick unto death. And Isaiah the prophet the son of Amoz came unto him, and said unto him, Thus saith the Lord, Set thine house in order: for thou shalt die, and not live. Then HEZEKIAH TURNED HIS FACE TOWARD THE WALL, AND PRAYED unto the Lord, [3] And said, Remember now, O Lord, I beseech thee, how I have walked before thee in truth and with a perfect heart, and have done that which is good in thy sight. And Hezekiah wept sore. [4] Then came the word of the Lord to Isaiah, saying, [5] Go, and say to Hezekiah, Thus saith the Lord, the God of David thy father, I HAVE HEARD THY PRAYER, I HAVE SEEN THY TEARS: BEHOLD, I WILL ADD UNTO THY DAYS FIFTEEN YEARS. And I will deliver thee and this city out of the hand of the king of Assyria: and I will defend this city.

Isaiah 38:1-6

Prayer is the altar of change! Through prayer, you will live longer. Hezekiah received a supernatural addition of years to his life.

God divinely added fifteen years to his life. There is no impossible case with God. God changed what He had decreed because of prayer.

Prayer changes things!

Prayer changed the prophecy of Hezekiah's death.

Prayer prolonged Hezekiah's life.

Prayer can change whatever man has said against you.

Prayer can change the effect of what man has said about you.

5.   Prayer changes things: Prayer changes threatening situations!

Fear thou not; for I am with thee: be not dismayed; for I am thy God: I will strengthen thee; yea, I will help thee; yea, I will uphold thee with the right hand of my righteousness. BEHOLD, ALL THEY THAT WERE INCENSED AGAINST THEE SHALL BE ASHAMED AND CONFOUNDED: THEY SHALL BE AS NOTHING; AND THEY THAT STRIVE WITH THEE SHALL PERISH. Thou shalt seek them, and shalt not find them, even them that contended with thee: they that war against thee shall be as nothing, and as a thing of nought.

Isaiah 41:10-12

Hezekiah was greatly threatened by the king of Assyria. Rashakeh, the agent of the king of Assyria, had come with a threatening intimidating and frightening message from the king of Assyria.

You're gonna die!

You're finished!

It is over!

Have you heard of anyone who survived this before?

You are not better than any of the kings of other nations.

You're gonna die! You are ruined!

Indeed, Hezekiah was unsettled and alarmed by the messages from Rabshakeh. I tell you, whatever message you have received that frightens and alarms you will not prosper and will not come to pass. Through prayer, you will be granted a divine escape from those who threaten you.

One day, I was in prayer when the Lord spoke to me directly from the Word. I had been hearing unsettling and alarming messages from various individuals. I kept wondering why some people hated me so much.

As I prayed, he gave me this amazing scripture. I knew it would come to pass exactly as he had said. All those who were incensed against me would be ashamed and confounded!

They shall be as nothing!

They that strive against thee shall perish.

You shall seek for them and you shall not fine them.

Truly, it came to pass practically!

Those who strove against me became as nothing.

They were ashamed and confounded!

They perished!   Prayer changes things!

Thus shall ye speak to Hezekiah king of Judah, saying, Let not thy God in whom thou trustest deceive thee, saying, Jerusalem shall not be delivered into the hand of the king of Assyria. Behold, thou hast heard what the kings of Assyria have done to all lands, by destroying them utterly: and shalt thou be delivered?

Have the gods of the nations delivered them which my fathers have destroyed; as Gozan, and Haran, and Rezeph, and the children of Eden which were in Thelasar? Where is the king of Hamath, and the king of Arpad, and the king of the city of Sepharvaim, of Hena, and Ivah? And Hezekiah received the letter of the hand of the messengers, and read it: and Hezekiah went up into the house of the Lord, and spread it before the Lord.

AND HEZEKIAH PRAYED BEFORE THE LORD, AND SAID, O LORD GOD OF ISRAEL, WHICH DWELLEST BETWEEN THE CHERUBIMS, THOU ART THE GOD, EVEN THOU ALONE, OF ALL THE KINGDOMS OF THE EARTH; THOU HAST MADE HEAVEN AND EARTH. Lord, bow down thine ear, and hear: open, Lord, thine eyes, and see: and hear the words of Sennacherib, which hath sent him to reproach the living God. Of a truth, Lord, the kings of Assyria have destroyed the nations and their lands, And have cast their gods into the fire: for they were no gods, but the work of men's hands, wood and stone: therefore they have destroyed them. Now therefore, O Lord our God, I beseech thee, save thou us out of his hand, that all the kingdoms of the earth may know that thou art the Lord God, even thou only.

THEN ISAIAH THE SON OF AMOZ SENT TO HEZEKIAH, SAYING, THUS SAITH THE LORD GOD OF ISRAEL, THAT WHICH THOU HAST PRAYED TO ME AGAINST SENNACHERIB KING OF ASSYRIA I HAVE HEARD. This is the word that the Lord hath spoken concerning him; The virgin the daughter of Zion hath despised thee, and laughed thee to scorn; the daughter of Jerusalem hath shaken her head at thee. Whom hast thou reproached and blasphemed? and against whom hast thou exalted thy voice, and lifted up thine eyes on high? even against the Holy One of Israel.

2 Kings 19:12-22

6. Prayer changes things: Prayer changes the outcome of sickness!

Now there was at Joppa a certain disciple named Tabitha, which by interpretation is called DORCAS: THIS WOMAN WAS FULL OF GOOD WORKS AND ALMSDEEDS WHICH SHE DID. AND IT CAME TO PASS IN THOSE DAYS, THAT SHE WAS SICK, AND DIED: whom when they had washed, they laid her in an upper chamber. And forasmuch as Lydda was nigh to Joppa, and the disciples had heard that Peter was there, they sent unto him two men, desiring him that he would not delay to come to them. Then Peter arose and went with them. When he was come, they brought him into the upper chamber: and all the widows stood by him weeping, and shewing the coats and garments which Dorcas made, while she was with them. BUT PETER PUT THEM ALL FORTH, AND KNEELED DOWN, AND PRAYED; AND TURNING HIM TO THE BODY SAID, TABITHA, ARISE. AND SHE OPENED HER EYES: and when she saw Peter, she sat up. And he gave her his hand, and lifted her up, and when he had called the saints and widows, presented her alive.

Acts 9:36-41

Prayer changes things! Prayer changed the outcome of sickness! Prayer will change the outcome of your sickness. Whatever disease you have; expect a great change in the outcome because of your prayers.

Dorcas was sick and eventually died. Many sicknesses lead to death. Prayer changed the outcome of Dorcas' illness.

I remember a vision that Kenneth Hagin had. The Lord told him that it was important to always pray for people in hospital. The Lord said to him that prayer would always alter the outcome of medical treatment. In the vision, it was clear that when people are in the hospital and they are prayed for, there would be some kind of change. Sometimes, things are determined and the person has to die. Prayer can change that. Prayer can delay death. Prayer can cancel the appointment with death and reschedule it for a much later date. Prayer changes things!

7. **Prayer changes things: Prayer silences all your mockers!**

Prayer changed a barren situation into a fruitful one. Hannah's destiny was changed by her prayer. The prayer of Hannah is connected to the story of Hannah. You can never tell the story of Hannah without talking about how she prayed in the temple. Hannah had nothing else to do than to trust in the Lord. Hannah was surrounded by mockers and scoffers. "Are there not mockers with me? and doth not mine eye continue in their provocation?" (Job 17:2)

Those who mock you will join you to celebrate with you. Prayer changes things! Prayer will cause all your mockers to be silenced. Expect a change as you pray today. Prayer changes things! Prayer will change your barren church into a fruitful one. Prayer will change your barren life into a fruitful one. As you spend time in prayer, the power of fruitfulness is released on you.

So Hannah rose up after they had eaten in Shiloh, and after they had drunk. Now Eli the priest sat upon a seat by a post of the temple of the Lord. AND SHE WAS IN BITTERNESS OF SOUL, AND PRAYED UNTO THE LORD, AND WEPT SORE. And she vowed a vow, and said, O Lord of hosts, if thou wilt indeed look on the affliction of thine handmaid, and remember me, and not forget thine handmaid, but wilt give unto thine handmaid a man child, then I will give him unto the Lord all the days of his life, and there shall no razor come upon his head.

And it came to pass, as she continued praying before the Lord, that Eli marked her mouth.

Now Hannah, she spake in her heart; only her lips moved, but her voice was not heard: therefore Eli thought she had been drunken. And Eli said unto her, How long wilt thou be drunken? Put away thy wine from thee. And Hannah answered and said, No, my lord, I am a woman of a sorrowful spirit: I have drunk neither wine nor strong drink, but have poured out my soul before the Lord. Count not thine handmaid for a daughter of Belial: for out of the abundance of my complaint and grief have I spoken hitherto.

THEN ELI ANSWERED AND SAID, GO IN PEACE: AND THE GOD OF ISRAEL GRANT THEE THY PETITION THAT THOU HAST ASKED OF HIM. AND SHE SAID, LET THINE HANDMAID FIND GRACE IN THY SIGHT. So the woman went her way, and did eat, and her countenance was no more sad. And they rose up in the morning early, and worshipped before the Lord, and returned, and came to their house to Ramah: and Elkanah knew Hannah his wife; and the Lord remembered her.

1 Samuel 1:9-19

8. Prayer changes things: Prayer changes the heavens over your life!

Elias was a man subject to like passions as we are, and he prayed earnestly that it might not rain: and it rained not on the earth by the space of three years and six months. And he prayed again, and the heaven gave rain, and the earth brought forth her fruit.

James 5:17-18

Prayer is the game changer. Prayer opens the heavens over you. Elijah was living under a brazen heaven that was yielding no blessings, no water and no rain. Nothing was working! Nothing was happening! Is it the case in your life that nothing is working and nothing is happening?

Is your church failing? Is your ministry going down? Prayer changes things! Prayer will open the heavens above and revelation will come to you.

Light will come to you as you pray. Expect a change as you pray. Prayer will also change your finances. Finances are controlled by heaven. The windows of heaven control the blessings that come into your life. If there is no open heaven, there will be no blessings for you. Through prayer, the cankerworms and the demonic locusts will be paralyzed in your life

Prayer changes things! Prayer will change everything for you. Prayer will open the heavens above your head. It is time to believe that prayer will change the spiritual climate in your life. Prayer will remove the curse that has introduced hardness, suffering, pain, emptiness, dryness, barrenness and desolation into your life.

CHAPTER 2

Prayer is Your Great Strength

And it came to pass afterward, that he loved a woman in the valley of Sorek, whose name *was* Delilah. And THE LORDS OF THE PHILISTINES came up unto her, and said unto her, Entice him, and see wherein his great strength *lieth*, and by what *means* we may prevail against him, that we may bind him to afflict him: and we will give thee every one of us eleven hundred *pieces* of silver.

And Delilah said to Samson, TELL ME, I PRAY THEE, WHEREIN THY GREAT STRENGTH LIETH, and wherewith thou mightest be bound to afflict thee.

Judges 16:4-6

S atan is looking for the source of your great supernatural strength. Prayer is the source of your great strength! When you spend time in prayer, you become anointed and begin to move in the supernatural. Prayer is the key to rising above human abilities and human strength. That is why Jesus told the disciples to pray in the Garden of Gethsemane. He wanted them to be powerful in the face of difficulty and tragedy.

In every war, your great strength is the targeted by the enemy. This is why arms depots, dams, electric installations, oil rigs, supply chains and even food sources are targeted by the enemy. Everything that provides sustenance for your enemy is a source of his strength. If you attack the source of his strength the enemy cannot fight back. In every spiritual war, satan is after your prayer life. Your prayer life is the source of your strength.

The Israelites were the people of God just as we are the people of God today. The lords of the Philistines were the enemies of the children of Israel. These Philistines therefore represent the principalities, the princes and the powers of darkness that war against believers today. There are three things you must learn from this revelation of the enemies of the children of God.

1.   Your enemies of God are made up of organised princes, rulers and authorities.

Make no mistake about it! Your enemies are organised princes, principalities and rulers. Meetings are held in the spirit realm to discuss how your life can be attacked and destroyed.

2.   The enemy has targeted leaders.

Certain people are the targets of devils and demons. Samson was a judge in Israel. He was a target of the Philistines. Anyone who is a leader in the house of God is a target of devils and wicked spirits. Many of the things that are happening to you are planned attacks.

3. You are a target because you work for God.

Anyone who depopulates hell and wins souls is like Samson is a target. Samson was killing Philistines and depopulating the Philistine cities. You are a target of satan because of the work you do. Because you are a target, you are experiencing repeated attacks which others do not.

When Delilah asked Samson about the source of his power, it should have alerted him to the fact that he was in real danger. If this woman had wanted his money, it would have worked out much better for Samson. Delilah was not after money, silver or gold. Delilah did not want Samson to marry her. Delilah was not after Samson's heart. Delilah did not want Samson to love her. Delilah was not after love!

Delilah did not need the love of this powerful Israelite. She wanted the source of his power! When Delilah succeeded in getting the source of his power Samson was finished.

Let us now look at what exactly Samson lost when he gave up the source of his great strength. This is what happens to you when you give up the source of your power. When you give up praying, you will lose certain things. You lose the power, the strength, the presence and the grace of God. A look at what Samson lost reveals what you lose when you give up prayer! A look at what Samson lost reveals what you lose when you give up your source of strength and power. A look at what Samson lost reveals what you lose when you give up praying for hours.

What it Means to Lose Your Great Strength

1. Losing your great supernatural strength means that you lose the presence of God.

And she said, The Philistines be upon thee, Samson. And he awoke out of his sleep, and said, I will go out as at

15

other times before, and shake myself. And HE WIST NOT
THAT THE LORD WAS DEPARTED FROM HIM.

Judges 16:20

When Samson lost his great strength to Delilah, he lost the
presence of God. The presence of God is the great strength that
you have. When a pastor stops praying, he may still preach a
good message. The messages may be intelligently put together.
But the presence of God may be absent. If you watch Christian
television, you will see lots of good preaching. But do you feel
the presence of God? It takes the presence of God to achieve
anything. Without the presence of God, you cannot do much.
Jesus said, without me, you can do nothing.

2.   Losing your great supernatural strength means that
   you lose your natural strength.

And she said, The Philistines be upon thee, Samson. And
he awoke out of his sleep, and said, I WILL GO OUT AS
AT OTHER TIMES BEFORE, AND SHAKE MYSELF.
And he wist not that the Lord was departed from him. But
the Philistines took him, and put out his eyes, and brought
him down to Gaza, and bound him with fetters of brass;
and he did grind in the prison house.

Judges 16:20-21

Your physical strength is lost when you lose the strength of
God. You may not be aware of how much your spirit affects
your physical body. Indeed, the state of your spirit greatly affects
your physical strength. As the scripture says, the body without
the spirit is dead.

As soon as the spirit leaves the body, the heart stops beating,
the man stops breathing and the blood stops circulating.

This means that the spirit has a direct connection with your
heart, your lungs, your blood and all your other organs. This
is why when there is something wrong with you spiritually, it
shows up physically. This why when you are sick spiritually,
you can become sick physically. As soon as Samson made the

spiritual mistake, he lost his physical ability to combat a strong enemy. Don't give up your prayer life. It will even affect your physical strength.

3. Losing your great supernatural strength means that you lose your freedom.

But THE PHILISTINES TOOK HIM, and put out his eyes, and brought him down to Gaza, AND BOUND HIM WITH FETTERS OF BRASS; and he did grind in the prison house.

Judges 16:21

When Samson lost his great strength to Delilah, he also lost his freedom. He was no longer able to move about as he used to. When you lose your strength in the ministry, you will no longer be able to move from place to place as you used to. You will become restricted. You may think to yourself that no one is inviting you anymore. You may think to yourself, people are rejecting my ministry. But the truth is, you have lost your strength and are unable to go around as you used to.

It takes the power of God to freely go around from nation to nation. It takes the power of God to freely move around from church to church. Your lack of strength causes a restriction to your movement. Think about it carefully, why was Samson limited and restricted? He had lost his great strength! Why are you limited in your ministry today? Perhaps you have lost the great strength that God wanted you to have.

4. Losing your great supernatural strength means that you will lose your position.

Then his brethren and all the house of his father came down, and took him, and brought him up, and buried him between Zorah and Eshtaol in the burying place of Manoah his father. AND HE JUDGED ISRAEL TWENTY YEARS.

Judges 16:31

When you lose your great strength you end up losing your position with God. When you lose your great strength you end up losing your position with other important people. Your position in relation to God determines everything. Your position in relation to certain people determines many things. In the book of revelation, you see Jesus standing in the midst of the seven golden sticks. This vision is a revelation of Jesus's position relative to his churches. In a warning to his church, Jesus warned that he would change their position.

> Remember therefore from whence thou art fallen, and repent, and do the first works; or else I will come unto thee quickly, and will remove thy candlestick out of his place, except thou repent. "
>
> Revelation 2:5

Your position is everything. Those who are closer have a different viewpoint. Those who are closer hear better and see better. Those who are closer benefit more! Those who are closer have many unofficial manifestations of goodness and mercies!

There are many advantages that come with a closer position. When your position is changed, your life changes with it.

When Samson lost his great strength, he lost his position as a judge. He was no longer a judge but a prisoner of war. Do not give up your prayer life. If you give it up you will lose your valued position with all its benefits. You will even lose your position in relation to important people.

One day, I warned some of my ministry workers about their prayer life. I told them, "Prayer is very important. Don't give up your prayer life for other aspects of ministry." But they did not listen to me. I noticed how they gave time and attention to computers, to fieldwork and to other aspects of ministry. I was constantly concerned about their prayer lives. One day, Satan struck at these prayerless ministry workers and all of them lost their positions. Their lives changed drastically because they lost their valuable positions in relation to God and in relation to important people. Satan is after the great strength that you have through prayer. If he gets your strength, he will get your position!

5. Losing your great supernatural strength means that you will lose your glory.

And when Delilah saw that he had told her all his heart, she sent and called for the lords of the Philistines, saying, come up this once, for he hath shewed me all his heart. Then the lords of the Philistines came up unto her, and brought money in their hand. And she made him sleep upon her knees; and she called for a man, and SHE CAUSED HIM TO SHAVE OFF THE SEVEN LOCKS OF HIS HEAD; and she began to afflict him, and his strength went from him.

Judges 16:18-19

When you lose your great strength you end up losing the glory of your ministry. Samson's long hair was glorious. Delilah removed his glory with the help of another man. When you give up the source of your great strength, you are giving up the source of your glory.

What makes you glorious is a secret of strength. Samson's hair was the source of his power and also the source of his glory. It is important that you identify what is the source of your glory. What makes you nice? What makes you attractive? What makes people desire you? That is the source of your glory!

When you spend time in prayer, the power of the Holy Spirit comes upon you. The power of God in your life makes you glorious, makes people like you and makes people attracted to you. You can give up your computers, your staff meetings, your board meetings, your finance committee discussions but don't give up your prayer. It is prayer that makes you glorious. It is prayer that makes you truly beautiful, attractive, desirable and glorious.

6.   **Losing your great supernatural strength means that you will lose your sight.**

BUT THE PHILISTINES TOOK HIM, AND PUT OUT HIS EYES, and brought him down to Gaza, and bound him with fetters of brass; and he did grind in the prison house.

Judges 16:21

When you lose your great strength you end up losing your sight. Samson lost his eyes. He could not see anymore. What does this mean for you? Losing your sight means that you will not see certain things anymore. Perhaps God took you abroad and enabled you to see the sights of London, Paris, New York and Atlanta. When you lose your sight, you will not be allowed to see any such places anymore.

Because you have lost your sight, God will not allow you to see wonderful things, wonderful places and wonderful sights. I always consider it a privilege when God allows me to see certain things. I was privileged to see wonderful and beautiful nations like South Africa, Kenya, and Swaziland. Most people do not have the experience of seeing certain places in this life.

Losing your sight also involves losing the opportunity to have certain experiences. I have been blessed to see mega churches in different continents of the world. What a privilege it has been to see how a mega church is actually run. I have been blessed to meet certain apostles and prophets in this life. Seeing these great people in the flesh has been a great experience and a tremendous blessing for me. What God allows you to see is part of the blessing of sight.

7.   **Losing your great supernatural strength means that you will lose your life.**

And Samson called unto the Lord, and said, O Lord GOD, remember me, I pray thee, and strengthen me, I pray thee, only this once, O God, that I may be at once avenged of the Philistines for my two eyes.

20

And Samson took hold of the two middle pillars upon which the house stood, and on which it was borne up, of the one with his right hand, and of the other with his left.

And Samson said, LET ME DIE WITH THE PHILISTINES. And he bowed himself with all his might; and the house fell upon the lords, and upon all the people that were therein. So the dead which he slew at his death were more than they which he slew in his life.

Then his brethren and all the house of his father came down, and took him, and brought him up, and buried him between Zorah and Eshtaol in the burying place of Manoah his father. And he judged Israel twenty years.

Judges 16:28-31

When you lose your great strength you end up losing your life. You may lose your life because you do not pray when you are supposed to pray. Your life may depend on you being prayerful. Prayerlessness can cost you your life. Samson lost his life because he gave away the source of his strength. Your ministry is connected to your life. If you lose your ministry, you have lost your life. Fight to be a prayer warrior! Fight everything that takes away your ability to pray! Do anything to stay awake and continue praying as long as you need to! Your life depends on it! The source of your great supernatural strength is prayer! Therefore, the source of your life is your prayer!

CHAPTER 3

Mountain Prayers

And it came to pass about an eight days after these sayings, he took Peter and John and James, and went up into a mountain to pray. And as he prayed, the fashion of his countenance was altered, and his raiment was white and glistering. And, behold, there talked with him two men, which were Moses and Elias:

Luke 9:28-30

T he passage above reveals how Jesus Christ went to the mountain of Transfiguration for prayer. Great changes happened in His life because of this prayer time. These are the same changes that will happen to you when you pray. There are ten amazing steps and experiences that show you the progressive effect of prayer as Jesus experienced it in His time of prayer on the mountain.

A mountain speaks of a place where you wait on God. The mountain is the place where you spend quality time in prayer. You will have every experience that Jesus had on the mountain as you spend time praying to the Lord.

1. Pray in the mountains.

And it came to pass about an eight days after these sayings, he took Peter and John and James, and went up into a mountain to pray.

Luke 9:28

Notice how Jesus went all the way up to the mountain to pray. Remember that there were no cable cars in those days. It was a great effort to climb all the way into the mountains to pray. The journey to pray is a prayer in itself. There are many times I have heard God speaking to me whilst I was on my way to a mountain for prayer. God recognizes that all the preparations you are making are part of your efforts to speak to Him and to seek Him.

It is important to go away for prayer. There must be a place where you pray. You will soon notice that God meets you in that place every time you pray there. Jesus Christ went into the mountain to pray and you must also go to your mountain to pray.

One day, I heard the Holy Spirit tell me, "Find another mountain." Although I already had a place to pray, He was telling me to locate another place where I could spend time praying and waiting on God.

2. Prayer changes your appearance.

And as he prayed, the fashion of his countenance was altered, and his raiment was white and glistering.

Luke 9:29

Notice that prayer changed the appearance of Jesus. The fashion of his countenance was changed. Prayer makes you nicer. People are more attracted to you when you pray. When you are prayerful, people are drawn to you. Notice how the appearance of Jesus changed when they prayed. The reason why people do not come to your church is because you are not prayerful.

Your prayerlessness makes you unattractive. Prayerfulness makes you likeable, appealing, charming and interesting to your followers. You may not believe it. The appearance of your face will be transformed. Even if you are not naturally good-looking, many people will begin you find you attractive.

3. Prayer makes the Bible come alive. The Bible speaks to you.

And, behold, there talked with him two men, which were Moses and Elias:

Luke 9:30

As you pray, the Bible will come alive to you. Moses and Elias came alive to Jesus as he prayed. Moses and Elijah had died long ago. They had died over two thousand years before the day of Jesus Christ. Their bones could not even be found on earth. Yet, these characters came alive to Jesus and the disciples. Indeed, as you pray, many things you read in the Bible will become real and practical to you. Characters in the Bible will become real to you.

4. Prayer times will cause the Lord to speak to you about eternity.

Who appeared in glory, and spake of his decease which he should accomplish at Jerusalem.

Luke 9:31

As Jesus prayed, His thoughts centred on his death and on the beginning of eternity. His disciples had a very spiritual experience. Times of prayer always lead you towards eternal things. As you pray, earthly things will fade away. Your mind will increasingly move towards heaven and eternity. God will move your heart and your mind towards spiritual things.

The longer you pray, the more spiritual and eternally minded you become. People are earthly-minded because they do not pray. People are carnal because they do not pray. When you move into prayer, you move into spirituality. Stay away from being a carnal Christian. Bible study cannot give you the spiritual tone of heart of mind that prayer gives you.

5. Prayer will cause God to speak to you about what you are to accomplish.

Who appeared in glory, and spake of his decease which he should accomplish at Jerusalem.

Luke 9:31

As you pray, the Lord will speak to you about what you must accomplish. Jesus received instructions about what he had to accomplish. The deeper you go in prayer, the more you focus on your spiritual goals and vision. The call of God is real. Prayer will cause the Holy Spirit to speak to you about what you must accomplish for Him. The reason why you do not receive fresh directions from the Lord concerning your ministry is because you do not give yourself to prayer. The more you pray, the more you will have revelation and direction for your ministry.

6. Prayer makes you see the glory of God in your life.

But Peter and they that were with him were heavy with sleep: and when they were awake, they saw his glory, and the two men that stood with him.

Luke 9:32

25

Through prayer you will see the glory of God. Peter and the other disciples saw the glory of God on the mount of prayer. Do you want to see the beauty of God in your ministry? Do you want to see the glory of God in your church? Then be like Jesus and spend hours in prayer on a mountain. Do not wait for a crisis. It is time to wait on God now! Most people wait for some kind of crisis before they pray. Pray that you may see the glory of God

7. Prayer makes you feel like staying in the presence of God.

And it came to pass, as they departed from him, Peter said unto Jesus, Master, it is good for us to be here: and let us make three tabernacles; one for thee, and one for Moses, and one for Elias: not knowing what he said.

Luke 9:33

While he thus spake, there came a cloud, and overshadowed them: and they feared as they entered into the cloud.

Luke 9:34

Through prayer you will experience the presence of God. The cloud of glory came on the mountain where Jesus was praying. Do you want to see the cloud of glory practically in your life? Then spend time praying!

One day, I was praying on my mountain and I saw a white pillar going up towards heaven. I was shocked to see this amazing white pillar of smoke. I had prayed in this place many times but I never thought I would see anything like that. My eyes were wide open and there was the pillar of white smoke right in the centre of the room. When you spend time in prayer, you will see the glory of God.

8. Prayer makes you hear the voice of God.

And there came a voice out of the cloud, saying, This is my beloved Son: hear him. And when the voice was past,

Jesus was found alone. And they kept it close, and told no man in those days any of those things which they had seen.

Luke 9:35-36

You will hear the voice of God as you pray. The voice of God may not say what you think it should say. The voice of God will confirm you on your journey. You need to hear the voice of God continually. Without the voice of God you cannot know whether you are doing the right thing. You cannot say you heard the voice of God last year and so you do not need to hear his voice this year. God wants to speak to you all the time. God is ready to give you fresh revelation and direction for your life. God is ready to confirm whether you are on the right direction or not.

9. Prayer makes demons submit themselves to you and obey your commands.

And it came to pass, that on the next day, WHEN THEY WERE COME DOWN FROM THE HILL, much people met him. And, behold, a man of the company cried out, saying, Master, I beseech thee, look upon my son: for he is mine only child. And, lo, a spirit taketh him, and he suddenly crieth out; and it teareth him that he foameth again, and bruising him hardly departeth from him.

And I besought thy disciples to cast him out; and they could not. And Jesus answering said, O faithless and perverse generation, how long shall I be with you, and suffer you? Bring thy son hither. And as he was yet a coming, the devil threw him down, and tare him. And Jesus rebuked the unclean spirit, and healed the child, and delivered him again to his father.

Luke 9:37-42

When Jesus came down from the mountain, He immediately cast out devils. There was much authority and much power available because of his prayer time. Do you want demons to submit themselves to you? Do you want to experience the power of God? Prayer is the secret to power. Anyone who wants to see power must be prayerful. Power to cast out devils is given to those who pray.

10.   Prayer causes you to walk in mighty power of God. Through prayer you will experience miracles, signs and wonders.

And they were all amazed at the mighty power of God. But while they wondered every one at all things which Jesus did, he said unto his disciples,

Luke 9:43

Many people were amazed by the power of God. The power of God was manifested because Jesus spent many hours in prayer. Follow the pattern of prayer that releases power. The release of the power of God is a standard response to prayer.

Jesus did not pray about healing or any such thing. He went to the mountain to pray. After the prayer on the mountain, Jesus amazed people with the power of God. Do you want people to be amazed by the power of God in your ministry? Do you wonder why people find you so ordinary and powerless in the ministry? It is time to follow the ministry pattern of Jesus. Get yourself a mountain! Go there! Spend time in the presence of God! You will see every one of these ten steps manifesting practically in your life.

CHAPTER 4

Prayer Makes You Supernatural

Marvel not that I said unto thee, Ye must be born again. The wind bloweth where it listeth, and thou hearest the sound thereof, but canst not tell whence it cometh, and whither it goeth: SO IS EVERY ONE THAT IS BORN OF THE SPIRIT.

John 3:7-8

Everyone who is born again is supposed to be supernatural. Everyone born of the spirit is supposed to be like the wind which cannot be predicted. No one can tell what is going to happen with the wind. It may blow softly or it may turn into a storm. The wind can change direction at any time. This is the nature of wind - unpredictable, invisible and powerful.

Human beings are exactly the opposite. We are predictable, visible and weak! When Jesus said a born again person would be like the wind, He was prophesying that we would become supernatural through the new birth experience.

Prayer is the gateway to the supernatural. A person who is spiritual and prayerful has a supernatural dimension to his life. Every prayerful person has supernatural forces working for him. If you want to see the supernatural in your life, you must go deep into prayer. Every time you pray, supernatural things happen. Every time you pray, God supernaturally intervenes in your situation. Nothing takes its natural course any more. There is a supernatural outplaying of your circumstances. You must have great faith in prayer!

1.   **Prayer introduces a supernatural dimension to your life! Jesus prayed in the wilderness for forty days and nights. Prayer brought in the supernatural nature of Jesus' ministry.**

And Jesus returned in the power of the Spirit into Galilee: and there went out a fame of him through all the region round about.

And he taught in their synagogues, being glorified of all.

And he came to Nazareth, where he had been brought up: and, as his custom was, he went into the synagogue on the sabbath day, and stood up for to read.

And there was delivered unto him the book of the prophet Esaias. And when he had opened the book, he found the place where it was written,

The Spirit of the Lord is upon me, because he hath anointed me to preach the gospel to the poor; he hath sent me to heal the brokenhearted, to preach deliverance to the captives, and recovering of sight to the blind, to set at liberty them that are bruised,

And he closed the book, and he gave it again to the minister, and sat down. And the eyes of all them that were in the synagogue were fastened on him.

And all bare him witness, and wondered at the gracious words which proceeded out of his mouth. And they said, Is not this Joseph's son?

And the fame of him went out into every place of the country round about.

Luke 4:14-18, 20, 22, 37

The ministry of Jesus was filled with supernatural events. Whenever we think of Jesus, we think of a supernatural person. Even the words he spoke were supernatural. "The spirit of the Lord is upon me" is supernatural statement. "Healing the brokenhearted" is a declaration of supernatural intent. "Deliverance to the captives" is a declaration of supernatural intent. "Recovering of sight to the blind" is a declaration of supernatural power. "Setting at liberty them that are bruised" is a declaration of supernatural abilities. Indeed the supernatural ministry of Jesus Christ was released after he prayed.

Do you want to experience the supernatural life? Do you want your business and your ministry to follow a natural course? The natural course is fraught with difficulties and curses. You will be lifted up above the natural contours, difficulties, challenges, obstacles, road blocks, hurdles and curses through prayer. Prayer introduces supernatural dimensions in to your life. Expect a new supernatural dimension to work in your life. It is not natural to become famous. It is the supernatural power of God that can make you famous. Jesus became famous because there was a supernatural element in His life. "And the fame of him went out into every place of the country round about"

2.   Prayer introduces a supernatural dimension to your life!

Now when all the people were baptized, it came to pass, that Jesus also being baptized, and PRAYING, the heaven was opened, And the Holy Ghost descended in a bodily shape like a DOVE upon him, and a VOICE came from heaven, which said, Thou art my beloved Son; in thee I am well pleased.

Luke 3:21-22

Whilst Jesus was praying, a supernatural dove appeared and descended on Him. Prayer brought in the supernatural!

Prayer brought in the Holy Ghost in the form of a dove. Supernatural doves descend from heaven every time you pray. These doves are the anointing of the Holy Spirit. This is why people who are prayerful are more anointed than people who just do Bible studies. Thank God that you are listening to messages now. You also need to spend hours praying and calling on God. Through that you will be anointed.

I have not seen any man of God who is really anointed and does not pray. I have watched people preach and sensed a lack of anointing. Yes, their messages were intelligent, Word-based, witty, loaded with examples, illustrations and anecdotes. But none of these could compensate for the lack of the anointing in the message.

The word of God is actually a supernatural thing. The preaching of the cross is the power of God unto salvation. God has chosen the foolishness of preaching to save people. Yes, preaching may sound foolish but when it is anointed it changes lives.

3.   Prayer introduces a supernatural dimension to your life!   Prayer will introduce honour and glory from God.

For he received from God the Father honour and glory, when there came such a voice to him from the excellent glory, this is my beloved Son, in whom I am well pleased. And this voice which came from heaven we heard, when we were with him in the holy mount.

2 Peter 1:17-18

While Jesus prayed, a voice came down from heaven and affirmed Him. Jesus Christ was confirmed to be the Son of God by the voice that came from heaven. In 1988, I was living in a town called Suhum in Ghana. I had to be in this town for one month. I spent the day working in the hospital and doing all the duties of a medical student. I had come away from the big city and I felt separate from man and closer to God. I decided to do a little extra praying and waiting on God. In the night, I would pray whenever I could. I would always listen to preaching messages whilst I was praying.

One night, I started praying at about 8.00pm but fell asleep. I woke up again at about 3.00am. I continued praying and listening to the preaching of Kenneth Hagin in the background. He was preaching about demons and how they affect human beings today. Suddenly, in the middle of my prayer time, whilst on my knees I felt something jump into my belly.

I heard a voice in the room saying, "From today you can teach." My life was transformed in that instant. I received the anointing to teach whilst I was praying on my knees in Suhum. That is why you are reading this book now.

That can be the only explanation why I have published over thirty million books to date. I had no idea that anything like that was going to happen. I had no particular desire to receive anything special from the Lord. A simple habit of praying, reading my Bible and listening to messages yielded such a blessing to me. I received the honour and glory of my ministry in that moment.

You will also receive honour and glory as you spend time praying to the Lord. The lack of honour and the lack of glory in your ministry comes from a lack of praying.

4.   Prayer introduces a supernatural dimension to your life!   Prayer brought in the visions of Moses and Elijah.

And it came to pass about an eight days after these sayings, he took Peter and John and James, and went up into a mountain to pray. And as he prayed, the fashion of his countenance was altered, and his raiment was white and glistering. And, behold, there talked with him two men, which were Moses and Elias:

Luke 9:28-30

You will have more visions and dreams when you pray. Prayer introduces you to the supernatural dimension of visions and dreams. Daniel, the prophet, prayed to the Lord three times a day. Daniel went to prison because of his prayer life. Daniel's long prayers are recorded in the ninth chapter of the book of Daniel. Daniel is the one who received amazing visions and dreams. The supernatural dimension of visions and dreams are introduced into your life through your prayer life.

Another person who had a lot of supernatural visions is John the revelator. John was in the spirit on the Lord's Day when he received all the visions recorded in the book of Revelation. John was praying and waiting on the word of God on the isle of Patmos. "I John, who also am your brother, and companion in tribulation, and in the kingdom and patience of Jesus Christ, was in the isle that is called Patmos, for the word of God, and for the testimony of Jesus Christ" (Revelation 1:9). This will be your story as you wait on the Lord. The supernatural dimension of ministry with multiple visions and dreams will be introduced practically into your life, as you get deeper into prayer.

5.   Prayer introduces a supernatural dimension to your life!

And it came to pass about an eight days after these sayings, he took Peter and John and James, and WENT UP INTO A MOUNTAIN TO PRAY.

AND AS HE PRAYED, the fashion of his countenance was altered, and his raiment was white and glistering. And, behold, there talked with him two men, which were Moses and Elias: Who appeared in glory, and spake of his decease which he should accomplish at Jerusalem.

Luke 9:28-31

The prayer life of Jesus introduced the wonder of supernatural transfiguration and transformation. It is definitely a supernatural experience to see Moses and Elijah. Moses and Elijah lived and died thousands of years ago. Expect supernatural experiences and encounters to multiply as you serve the Lord in prayer.

As you serve the Lord in prayer, your appearance will supernaturally be transformed. People will try to blacken your image with bad stories and blasphemy. Yet, through prayers, you will be transformed and appear white, clean and glistening before those who matter. Not everyone's opinion about you matters. What God thinks about you is what matters. Those you are called to and those whose destiny is linked with yours is what matters.

6.   Prayer introduces a supernatural dimension to your life!   Prayer brought in great grace and great power.

And WHEN THEY HAD PRAYED, THE PLACE WAS SHAKEN WHERE THEY WERE ASSEMBLED TOGETHER; and they were all filled with the Holy Ghost, and they spake the word of God with boldness. And the multitude of them that believed were of one heart and of one soul: neither said any of them that ought of the things which he possessed was his own; but they had all things common.

And with GREAT POWER gave the apostles witness of the resurrection of the Lord Jesus: and GREAT GRACE was upon them all.

Acts 4:31-33

Prayer introduces great grace to your church. Great power and authority is a supernatural thing that can only come through prayer. Perhaps you are wondering why someone else's ministry seems to have such grace? The answer is prayer! Prayer is the key to receiving the undeserved help and favour from God. Even the answers to your prayer are undeserved. No matter how much you pray you still do not deserve an answer. Grace is the receiving of undeserved answers to your prayers.

CHAPTER 5

How You Can Secure Angelic Intervention

Prayer is the greatest and most definite way of securing angelic participation. Jesus, in the garden of Gethsemane, made this reality clear. Prayer is the way to guarantee angelic participation and intervention in your life. Jesus declared that He could easily pray and have twelve legions of angels (seventy-five thousand, four hundred and thirty-two angels.)

Then said Jesus unto him, Put up again thy sword into his place: for all they that take the sword shall perish with the sword. THINKEST THOU THAT I CANNOT NOW PRAY TO MY FATHER, AND HE SHALL PRESENTLY GIVE ME MORE THAN TWELVE LEGIONS OF ANGELS? But how then shall the scriptures be fulfilled, that thus it must be?

Matthew 26:52-54

Prayer Secures Angelic Intervention And Participation

We pray to secure angelic activity and angelic intervention.

You need angelic involvement in your life. Without angelic involvement, you will not be able to do many of the things that God has called you to do.

Without angelic intervention and participation, your life will follow the natural contours of the terrain. When everything is going down, you will go down! When everything is going up, you will go up. However, with angelic intervention, when everything is going down, you will still go up. Why is that? The angel has intervened and interrupted the natural course of events.

I am sure you want God to interrupt, intervene and move mightily in your life. You definitely need angelic participation and intervention in your life.

There are a number of things that angels will do for you. As you secure their participation, they will do what they are called to do in your life. Angels intervene to *keep you* and *bring you* to your destination.

> Behold, I send an Angel before thee, TO KEEP THEE IN THE WAY, and to bring thee into the place which I have prepared.
>
> Exodus 23:20

Another way that angels participate in your life is to speak to you. It is important to learn what it sounds like when an angel is speaking in your life.

Angels do many things. If you learn to accept the participation and the intervention of angels, you will find that they chase away your enemies. They become enemies to your enemies. Wouldn't you want your enemies to have a good enemy to fight and oppose them? Something that can match their wickedness toe-to-toe?

Behold, I send an Angel before thee, to keep thee in the way, and to bring thee into the place which I have prepared. BEWARE OF HIM, AND OBEY HIS VOICE, provoke him not; for he will not pardon your transgressions: for my name is in him. But if thou shalt indeed obey his voice, and do all that I speak; then I will be an enemy unto thine enemies, and an adversary unto thine adversaries.

Exodus 23:20-22

Angels can even release plagues and pandemics. Many plagues and pandemics of this world are caused by the activities of angels.

And I saw another sign in heaven, great and marvellous, SEVEN ANGELS HAVING THE SEVEN LAST PLAGUES; for in them is filled up the wrath of God.

Revelation 15:1

Since angels make such a difference to our lives, it is important to find a way to secure their participation in our lives. How can you secure angelic intervention and participation? There are a few well-known ways to bring an angel on board.

Hospitality and Entertainment Secure Angelic Intervention and Participation

The first well-known way of bringing angels into your life is through entertainment and hospitality. Angels love to be entertained. It seems that angels like food. The Scripture is very clear; *"Be not forgetful to entertain strangers: for thereby some have entertained angels unawares."* Angels love entertainment. They love welcoming people who cook, provide food and warmth for them. Many people who have entertained people didn't know that they were entertaining angels. These examples prove that hospitality is a way to introduce angelic intervention in your life and in your ministry.

Lot was very hospitable and entertained angels who later turned out to be his saviours.

39

And there came two angels to Sodom at even; and Lot sat in the gate of Sodom: and Lot seeing them rose up to meet them; and he bowed himself with his face toward the ground; And he said, Behold now, my lords, turn in, I pray you, into your servant's house, and tarry all night, and wash your feet, and ye shall rise up early, and go on your ways. And they said, Nay; but we will abide in the street all night. And he pressed upon them greatly; and they turned in unto him, and entered into his house; AND HE MADE THEM A FEAST, AND DID BAKE UNLEAVENED BREAD, AND THEY DID EAT.

Genesis 19:1-3

Abraham was very welcoming and hospitable. With great effort he provided food and drinks for his guests. These guests turned out to be angels who helped them to have a child. Angels seem to like food. They go where they are fed. They intervene and participate in the situation at hand.

And the Lord appeared unto him in the plains of Mamre: and he sat in the tent door in the heat of the day; And he lift up his eyes and looked, and, lo, three men stood by him: and when he saw them, he ran to meet them from the tent door, and bowed himself toward the ground, And said, My Lord, if now I have found favour in thy sight, pass not away, I pray thee, from thy servant: Let a little water, I pray you, be fetched, and wash your feet, and rest yourselves under the tree: And I will fetch a morsel of bread, and comfort ye your hearts; after that ye shall pass on: for therefore are ye come to your servant. And they said, So do, as thou hast said. And Abraham hastened into the tent unto Sarah, and said, Make ready quickly three measures of fine meal, knead it, and make cakes upon the hearth. And Abraham ran unto the herd, and fetch a calf tender and good, and gave it unto a young man; and he hasted to dress it. AND HE TOOK BUTTER, AND MILK, AND THE CALF WHICH HE HAD DRESSED, AND SET IT

BEFORE THEM; AND HE STOOD BY THEM UNDER
THE TREE, AND THEY DID EAT.

Genesis 18:1-8

Manoah, the father of Samson, was also a hospitable man.
Unlike some Christians to day, he was happy to host visitors and
provide food for them. He commanded his wife to cheerfully
cook for the visitors. Because of his hospitality, angels were
attracted to his residence.

AND MANOAH SAID UNTO THE ANGEL OF THE
LORD, I PRAY THEE, LET US DETAIN THEE, UNTIL
WE SHALL HAVE MADE READY A KID FOR THEE.
And the angel of the Lord said unto Manoah, Though
thou detain me, I will not eat of thy bread: and if thou wilt
offer a burnt offering, thou must offer it unto the Lord.
For Manoah knew not that he was an angel of the Lord.
And Manoah said unto the angel of the Lord, What is thy
name, that when thy sayings come to pass we may do thee
honour? And the angel of the Lord said unto him, Why
askest thou thus after my name, seeing it is secret?

So Manoah took a kid with a meat offering, and offered it
upon a rock unto the Lord: and the angel did wondrously;
and Manoah and his wife looked on. For it came to pass,
when the flame went up toward heaven from off the altar,
that the angel of the Lord ascended in the flame of the
altar. And Manoah and his wife looked on it, and fell on
their faces to the ground. But the angel of the Lord did
no more appear to Manoah and to his wife. Then Manoah
knew that he was an angel of the Lord.

Judges 13:15-21

Being A Servant Secures Angelic Intervention and Participation

And it came to pass, that while he executed the priest's
office before God in the order of his course, According to
the custom of the priest's office, his lot was to burn incense

41

when he went into the temple of the Lord. And the whole multitude of the people were praying without at the time of incense. And there appeared unto him an angel of the Lord standing on the right side of the altar of incense. And when Zacharias saw him, he was troubled, and fear fell upon him.

Luke 1:8-12

Being a servant of God is the second way to interact with angels. Comrades meet naturally and interact freely! When you become a servant of God you will be forced to encounter and interact with co-servants.

People who do not make themselves the servants of God will never have the privilege of encountering other fellow servants. In a large mansion the butler, the housekeeper, the security guards, the cleaners, the chef, the cook, the maidservants and the manservants interact freely. They even have a common space where they fellowship together.

Decide to become a servant of God! You will interact freely with angels. You will experience their participation and intervention! As Zacharias served the Lord and executed the priest's office, an angel appeared to him. It is natural that servants interact all the time. Expect to interact with angels! They are your fellow servants!

Fearing God Secures Angelic Intervention and Participation

Fearing God is another master key to securing the presence, participation and intervention of angels.

The angel of the Lord encampeth round about THEM THAT FEAR HIM, and delivereth them.

Psalm 34:7

The Word Secures Angelic Intervention and Participation

Angels love the word of God. Angels hearken to the sound of the Word of God. Speaking the Word of God is a sure way to attract angels. Angels come anywhere there is the sound of preaching. Angels attend church services, crusades, breakfast meetings, conventions and seminars just to hear the Word of God. You will find angels wherever the good word of God is preached. Notice what the scripture says,

> Bless the Lord, ye his angels, that excel in strength, that do his commandments, HEARKENING UNTO THE VOICE OF HIS WORD.

> Psalm 103:20

When you confess and declare the word of God, angels will be attracted from far away galaxies. They will come from far and wide to participate in the joy, truth and power of God's Word.

CHAPTER 6

Prayer Secures Angelic Intervention and Participation

Thinkest thou that I cannot now PRAY to my Father, and he shall presently give me more than twelve legions of angels? But how then shall the scriptures be fulfilled, that thus it must be?

Matthew 26:53-54

All through the Bible, you see angels appearing wherever people prayed. Jesus made it clear that prayer was the way to involve angels in your life. He declared that he could have deployed as many as seventy-five thousand angels if He prayed for them. I want you to see how often angels are released because of people's prayers. It is almost like magic. There is a prayer and then there is an angel!

Where there is prayer there is angel intervention and angelic activity. Prayer activates and releases angels! Prayers stir up Angel activity! Where there is prayer, there is increased angel activity. Where there is increased angelic activity, there are increased supernatural occurrences.

1. PRAYER SECURED ANGELIC INTERVENTION FOR ZACHARIAH.

Notice the words of the angel who appeared to Zachariah. "Fear not, Zacharias. Your prayer is heard!" Angels were sent to Zachariah because he prayed. An angel was finally intervening in Zachariah's life because of his prayer.

Expect angelic intervention because of your many prayers. Your heart's desire will be answered by the intervention of angels. Your lifelong dream will come to pass because you prayed.

And it came to pass, that while he executed the priest's office before God in the order of his course, According to the custom of the priest's office, his lot was to burn incense when he went into the temple of the Lord. And the whole multitude of the people were praying without at the time of incense. AND THERE APPEARED UNTO HIM AN ANGEL OF THE LORD STANDING ON THE RIGHT SIDE OF THE ALTAR OF INCENSE. And when Zacharias saw him, he was troubled, and fear fell upon him. But the angel said unto him, FEAR NOT, ZACHARIAS: FOR THY PRAYER IS HEARD; and thy wife Elisabeth shall bear thee a son, and thou shalt call his name John.

And thou shalt have joy and gladness; and many shall rejoice at his birth. For he shall be great in the sight of the Lord, and shall drink neither wine nor strong drink; and he shall be filled with the Holy Ghost, even from his mother's womb. And many of the children of Israel shall he turn to the Lord their God.

Luke 1:8-16

2. PRAYER SECURED ANGELIC INTERVENTION FOR PETER.

Through prayer, Angels intervened in Peter's ministry when he was put in prison. Expect angels to cause the impossible breakthrough you need.

Now about that time Herod the king stretched forth his hands to vex certain of the church. And he killed James the brother of John with the sword.

And because he saw it pleased the Jews, he proceeded further to take Peter also. (Then were the days of unleavened bread.)

And when he had apprehended him, he put him in prison, and delivered him to four quaternions of soldiers to keep him; intending after Easter to bring him forth to the people.

PETER THEREFORE WAS KEPT IN PRISON: BUT PRAYER WAS MADE WITHOUT CEASING OF THE CHURCH UNTO GOD FOR HIM.

And when Herod would have brought him forth, the same night Peter was sleeping between two soldiers, bound with two chains: and the keepers before the door kept the prison. AND, BEHOLD, THE ANGEL OF THE LORD CAME UPON HIM, and a light shined in the prison: and he smote Peter on the side, and raised him up, saying, arise up quickly. And his chains fell off from his hands.

And the angel said unto him, Gird thyself, and bind on thy sandals. And so he did. And he saith unto him, Cast thy garment about thee, and follow me.

46

And he went out, and followed him; and wist not that it was true which was done by the angel; but thought he saw a vision.

When they were past the first and the second ward, they came unto the iron gate that leadeth unto the city; which opened to them of his own accord: and they went out, and passed on through one street; and forthwith the angel departed from him.

And when Peter was come to himself, he said, Now I know of a surety, that the Lord hath sent his angel, and hath delivered me out of the hand of Herod, and from all the expectation of the people of the Jews.

And when he had considered the thing, he came to the house of Mary the mother of John, whose surname was Mark; where many were gathered together praying.

Acts 12:1-12

3. PRAYER CAUSED ANGELIC INTERVENTION FOR CORNELIUS.

Through prayer, Angels intervened in Cornelius' life. Expect angels to respond to your prayers by appearing and getting involved in the situation. Cornelius received the Holy Spirit through the intervention of the angel. Through the activity of the angel, Cornelius was led to salvation. Through the activity of the angel, Cornelius was led to God's man. You will always find angels where there are prayerful people.

There was a certain man in Caesarea called CORNELIUS, a centurion of the band called the Italian band,

A DEVOUT MAN, AND ONE THAT FEARED GOD with all his house, which gave much alms to the people, and PRAYED TO GOD ALWAY.

HE SAW IN A VISION EVIDENTLY ABOUT THE NINTH HOUR OF THE DAY AN ANGEL OF GOD COMING IN TO HIM, and saying unto him, Cornelius.

And when he looked on him, he was afraid, and said, What is it, Lord? And he said unto him, Thy prayers and thine alms are come up for a memorial before God.

And now send men to Joppa, and call for one Simon, whose surname is Peter:

He lodgeth with one Simon a tanner, whose house is by the sea side: he shall tell thee what thou oughtest to do.

Acts 10:1-6

4. PRAYER SECURED ANGELIC PARTICIPATION FOR PAUL.

Through prayer, Angels intervened in Paul's shipwreck. Where there is prayer there is always angel intervention and angelic activity. Paul's prayers in the ship released an angel of deliverance. Your deliverance angel is released now.

And we being exceedingly tossed with a tempest, the next day they lightened the ship; And the third day we cast out with our own hands the tackling of the ship.

And when neither sun nor stars in many days appeared, and no small tempest lay on us, all hope that we should be saved was then taken away.

BUT AFTER LONG ABSTINENCE PAUL STOOD FORTH IN THE MIDST OF THEM, and said, Sirs, ye should have hearkened unto me, and not have loosed from Crete, and to have gained this harm and loss.

And now I exhort you to be of good cheer: for there shall be no loss of any man's life among you, but of the ship.

FOR THERE STOOD BY ME THIS NIGHT THE ANGEL OF GOD, WHOSE I AM, AND WHOM I SERVE,

SAYING, FEAR NOT, PAUL; THOU MUST BE BROUGHT BEFORE CAESAR: AND, LO, GOD HATH GIVEN THEE ALL THEM THAT SAIL WITH THEE.

Wherefore, sirs, be of good cheer: for I believe God, that it shall be even as it was told me.

Acts 27:18-25

5. PRAYER CAUSED ANGELIC INTERVENTION AND PARTICIPATION FOR DANIEL.

Through prayer, angels intervened in Daniel's life and ministry. Where there is prayer there is angelic intervention and increased angel activity. Daniel's prayers for Israel immediately caused angels to be released from heaven. You will notice that as soon as the supplications and prayers began, a commandment for the deployment of angelic forces was issued.

YEA, WHILES I WAS SPEAKING IN PRAYER, EVEN THE MAN GABRIEL, whom I had seen in the vision at the beginning, being caused to fly swiftly, touched me about the time of the evening oblation.

And he informed me, and talked with me, and said, O Daniel, I am now come forth to give thee skill and understanding.

AT THE BEGINNING OF THY SUPPLICATIONS THE COMMANDMENT CAME FORTH, AND I AM COME TO SHEW THEE; FOR THOU ART GREATLY BELOVED: therefore understand the matter, and consider the vision.

Seventy weeks are determined upon thy people and upon thy holy city, to finish the transgression, and to make an end of sins, and to make reconciliation for iniquity, and to bring in everlasting righteousness, and to seal up the vision and prophecy, and to anoint the most Holy.

Know therefore and understand, that from the going forth of the commandment to restore and to build Jerusalem unto the Messiah the Prince shall be seven weeks, and threescore and two weeks: the street shall be built again, and the wall, even in troublous times.

Daniel 9:21-25

6. PRAYER CAUSES ANGELIC INTERVENTION AND PARTICIPATION FOR SAINTS.

Through prayer, angels offered up incense to God. Where there is prayer there is angelic activity. When your prayers come up to heaven angels are forced to offer incense with them. Angels are also forced to throw fire down on earth in response to prayers. Angels are thrown into frenzied activity when you start praying.

And I saw the seven angels which stood before God; and to them were given seven trumpets. AND ANOTHER ANGEL CAME AND STOOD AT THE ALTAR, HAVING A GOLDEN CENSER; AND THERE WAS GIVEN UNTO HIM MUCH INCENSE, THAT HE SHOULD OFFER IT WITH THE PRAYERS OF ALL SAINTS UPON THE GOLDEN ALTAR which was before the throne. And the smoke of the incense, which came with the prayers of the saints, ascended up before God out of the angel's hand. And the angel took the censer, and filled it with fire of the altar, and cast it into the earth: and there were voices, and thunderings, and lightnings, and an earthquake.

Revelation 8:2-5

Zion is the house of God. Coming to God's house, the house of prayer is to come to an increased activity of an innumerable company of angels with their activities. The house of God is the house of prayer. And it shall come to pass in the last days, that the mountain of the LORD'S house shall be established in the top of the mountains, and shall be exalted above the hills; and all nations shall flow unto it.

"And many people shall go and say, Come ye, and let us go up to the mountain of the LORD, to the house of the God of Jacob; and he will teach us of his ways, and we will walk in his paths: for out of Zion shall go forth the law, and the word of the LORD from Jerusalem." (Isaiah 2:2-3). As you approach Mount Zion in prayer, you discover an innumerable company of angels. Seeking God, seeking

Mount Zion, praying to the Lord causes you to encounter many angels.

BUT YE ARE COME UNTO MOUNT SION, and unto the city of the living God, the heavenly Jerusalem, and TO AN INNUMERABLE COMPANY OF ANGELS, To the general assembly and church of the firstborn, which are written in heaven, and to God the Judge of all, and to the spirits of just men made perfect, And to Jesus the mediator of the new covenant, and to the blood of sprinkling, that speaketh better things than that of Abel.

Hebrews 12:22-24

7. PRAYER CAUSES ANGELIC INTERVENTION IN THE LIFE OF HAGAR.

Prayer releases angels. Hagar's cry was heard. Hagar's affliction was noticed! God sent an angel who gave her solid advise of humility. Angels will bring you good humble advice. Angels will appear in the midst of your crisis and help you greatly

Then Sarai said to Abram, "This is all your fault! I put my servant into your arms, but now that she's pregnant she treats me with contempt. The Lord will show who's wrong—you or me!" Abram replied, "Look, she is your servant, so deal with her as you see fit." Then Sarai treated Hagar so harshly that she finally ran away. The angel of the LORD found Hagar beside a spring of water in the wilderness, along the road to Shur. The angel said to her, "Hagar, Sarai's servant, where have you come from, and where are you going?" "I'm running away from my mistress, Sarai," she replied. The angel of the LORD said to her, "Return to your mistress, and submit to her authority." THEN HE ADDED, "I WILL GIVE YOU MORE DESCENDANTS THAN YOU CAN COUNT." AND THE ANGEL ALSO SAID, "YOU ARE NOW PREGNANT AND WILL GIVE BIRTH TO A SON. YOU ARE TO NAME HIM ISHMAEL (WHICH MEANS 'GOD HEARS'), FOR THE LORD HAS HEARD YOUR

CRY OF DISTRESS. This son of yours will be a wild man, as untamed as a wild donkey! He will raise his fist against everyone, and everyone will be against him. Yes, he will live in open hostility against all his relatives." Thereafter, Hagar used another name to refer to the LORD, who had spoken to her. She said, "You are the God who sees me." She also said, "Have I truly seen the One who sees me?"

Genesis 16:5-13 (NLT)

And the angel also said, "You are now pregnant and will give birth to a son. You are to name him Ishmael (which means 'God hears'), for the LORD has heard your cry of distress.

Genesis 26:11 (NLT)

8. PRAYER SECURES ANGELIC INTERVENTION AND PARTICIPATION FOR ABRAHAM.

Angels were deployed immediately after Abraham's prayer to the Lord for Sodom and Gomorrah. Prayer releases angels. Angel activity increases when there is prayer. The release of angels is a rule and a heavenly response to all serious prayers. As soon as Abraham prayed and interceded for Sodom, God sent angels there. The Intercession of Abraham is the last verse in the eighteenth chapter of Genesis. In the very next verse, we see angels appearing in the house of Lot.

AND HE SAID, OH LET NOT THE LORD BE ANGRY, AND I WILL SPEAK YET BUT THIS ONCE: PERADVENTURE TEN SHALL BE FOUND THERE. AND HE SAID, I WILL NOT DESTROY IT FOR TEN'S SAKE. And the Lord went his way, as soon as he had left communing with Abraham: and Abraham returned unto his place.

Genesis 18:32-33

AND THERE CAME TWO ANGELS TO SODOM AT EVEN; and Lot sat in the gate of Sodom: and Lot seeing them rose up to meet them; and he bowed himself with his face toward the ground; And he said, Behold now, my lords, turn in, I pray you, into your servant's house, and tarry all night, and wash your feet, and ye shall rise up early, and go on your ways. And they said, Nay; but we will abide in the street all night. And he pressed upon them greatly; and they turned in unto him, and entered into his house; and he made them a feast, and did bake unleavened bread, and they did eat.

Genesis 19:1-3

9. PRAYER SECURED ANGELIC INTERVENTION AND PARTICIPATION FOR JACOB.

Prayer releases angels. Jacob encountered an angel when he prayed all night. Jacob's prayers released angels of empowerment. Angel activity is always found around men who pray to God. Jacob was empowered to become the great nation of Israel by the angel he encountered at Peniel.

AND JACOB WAS LEFT ALONE; AND THERE WRESTLED A MAN WITH HIM UNTIL THE BREAKING OF THE DAY.

And when he saw that he prevailed not against him, he touched the hollow of his thigh; and the hollow of Jacob's thigh was out of joint, as he wrestled with him.

And he said, Let me go, for the day breaketh. And he said, I will not let thee go, except thou bless me.

And he said unto him, what is thy name? And he said, Jacob.

AND HE SAID, THY NAME SHALL BE CALLED NO MORE JACOB, BUT ISRAEL: FOR AS A PRINCE HAST THOU POWER WITH GOD AND WITH MEN, AND HAST PREVAILED.

And Jacob asked him, and said, Tell me, I pray thee, thy name. And he said, Wherefore is it that thou dost ask after my name? And he blessed him there.

53

And Jacob called the name of the place Peniel: for I have seen God face to face, and my life is preserved.

Genesis 32:24-30

10. PRAYER SECURES ANGELIC INTERVENTION FOR MOSES.

Prayer causes angel activities to happen in the life and ministry of Moses. Moses prayers released angels to help and guide the children of Israel out of Egypt. The Israelites were brought out of Egypt by an angel. That angel came in response to a prayer.

And Moses sent messengers from Kadesh unto the king of Edom, Thus saith thy brother Israel, Thou knowest all the travail that hath befallen us: How our fathers went down into Egypt, and we have dwelt in Egypt a long time; and the Egyptians vexed us, and our fathers: AND WHEN WE CRIED UNTO THE LORD, HE HEARD OUR VOICE, AND SENT AN ANGEL, AND HATH BROUGHT US FORTH OUT OF EGYPT: and, behold, we are in Kadesh, a city in the uttermost of thy border: Let us pass, I pray thee, through thy country: we will not pass through the fields, or through the vineyards, neither will we drink of the water of the wells: we will go by the king's high way, we will not turn to the right hand nor to the left, until we have passed thy borders.

Numbers 20:14-17

11. PRAYER SECURES ANGELIC INTERVENTION AND PARTICIPATION FOR ELIJAH.

Angel activity is increased by prayers. Elijah enjoyed the presence of angels in the midst of his crisis. These angels came on the scene because of Elijah's prayers. Elijah prayed to die but he fell asleep and was woken up by an angel. The angel did not leave Elijah all through the time he was depressed. The angel of the Lord was sent to help Elijah in his depressed and suicidal state. Prayer secures angelic participation. As you can see, it is almost like magic. There is a prayer and then there is an angel!

And Ahab told Jezebel all that Elijah had done, and withal how he had slain all the prophets with the sword.

Then Jezebel sent a messenger unto Elijah, saying, So let the gods do to me, and more also, if I make not thy life as the life of one of them by to morrow about this time.

And when he saw that, he arose, and went for his life, and came to Beer-sheba, which belongeth to Judah, and left his servant there.

But he himself went a day's journey into the wilderness, and came and sat down under a juniper tree: AND HE REQUESTED FOR HIMSELF THAT HE MIGHT DIE; AND SAID, IT IS ENOUGH; NOW, O LORD, TAKE AWAY MY LIFE; FOR I AM NOT BETTER THAN MY FATHERS.

AND AS HE LAY AND SLEPT UNDER A JUNIPER TREE, BEHOLD, THEN AN ANGEL TOUCHED HIM, AND SAID UNTO HIM, ARISE AND EAT.

And he looked, and, behold, there was a cake baken on the coals, and a cruse of water at his head. And he did eat and drink, and laid him down again.

And the angel of the Lord came again the second time, and touched him, and said, Arise and eat; because the journey is too great for thee.

1 Kings 19:1-7

12. PRAYER SECURES ANGELIC INTERVENTION FOR HEZEKIAH.

An Angel was sent to intervene in the war because of the prayers of Hezekiah. Angels are released to execute judgment on your enemy. Do not stop praying. Prayer secures angelic activity. Angels will destroy all your mockers. Angels will fight those who are fighting against you. Angels will contend against those who are contending against you.

And it came to pass, when king Hezekiah heard it, that he rent his clothes, and covered himself with sackcloth, and went into the house of the Lord.

And he sent Eliakim, which was over the household, and Shebna the scribe, and the elders of the priests, covered with sackcloth, to Isaiah the prophet the son of Amoz.

And they said unto him, Thus saith Hezekiah, This day is a day of trouble, and of rebuke, and blasphemy: for the children are come to the birth, and there is not strength to bring forth.

It may be the Lord thy God will hear all the words of Rab-shakeh, whom the king of Assyria his master hath sent to reproach the living God; and will reprove the words which the Lord thy God hath heard: WHEREFORE LIFT UP THY PRAYER FOR THE REMNANT THAT ARE LEFT.

So the servants of king Hezekiah came to Isaiah.

And Isaiah said unto them, Thus shall ye say to your master, Thus saith the Lord, Be not afraid of the words which thou hast heard, with which the servants of the king of Assyria have blasphemed me.

Behold, I will send a blast upon him, and he shall hear a rumour, and shall return to his own land; and I will cause him to fall by the sword in his own land.

So Rab-shakeh returned, and found the king of Assyria warring against Libnah: for he had heard that he was departed from Lachish.

And when he heard say of Tirhakah king of Ethiopia, Behold, he is come out to fight against thee: he sent messengers again unto Hezekiah, saying,

Thus shall ye speak to Hezekiah king of Judah, saying, Let not thy God in whom thou trustest deceive thee, saying, Jerusalem shall not be delivered into the hand of the king of Assyria.

Behold, thou hast heard what the kings of Assyria have done to all lands, by destroying them utterly: and shalt thou be delivered?

Have the gods of the nations delivered them which my fathers have destroyed; as Gozan, and Haran, and Rezeph, and the children of Eden which were in Thelasar?

Where is the king of Hamath, and the king of Arpad, and the king of the city of Sepharvaim, of Hena, and Ivah?

And Hezekiah received the letter of the hand of the messengers, and read it: and Hezekiah went up into the house of the Lord, and spread it before the Lord.

AND HEZEKIAH PRAYED BEFORE THE LORD, AND SAID, O LORD GOD OF ISRAEL, WHICH DWELLEST BETWEEN THE CHERUBIMS, THOU ART THE GOD, EVEN THOU ALONE, OF ALL THE KINGDOMS OF THE EARTH; THOU HAST MADE HEAVEN AND EARTH.

LORD, BOW DOWN THINE EAR, AND HEAR: OPEN, LORD, THINE EYES, AND SEE: AND HEAR THE WORDS OF SENNACHERIB, WHICH HATH SENT HIM TO REPROACH THE LIVING GOD.

OF A TRUTH, LORD, THE KINGS OF ASSYRIA HAVE DESTROYED THE NATIONS AND THEIR LANDS,

AND HAVE CAST THEIR GODS INTO THE FIRE: FOR THEY WERE NO GODS, BUT THE WORK OF MEN'S HANDS, WOOD AND STONE: THEREFORE THEY HAVE DESTROYED THEM.

NOW THEREFORE, O LORD OUR GOD, I BESEECH THEE, SAVE THOU US OUT OF HIS HAND, THAT ALL THE KINGDOMS OF THE EARTH MAY KNOW THAT THOU ART THE LORD GOD, EVEN THOU ONLY.

Then Isaiah the son of Amoz sent to Hezekiah, saying, Thus saith the Lord God of Israel, That which thou hast prayed to me against Sennacherib king of Assyria I have heard.

This is the word that the Lord hath spoken concerning him; The virgin the daughter of Zion hath despised thee, and laughed thee to scorn; the daughter of Jerusalem hath shaken her head at thee.

Whom hast thou reproached and blasphemed? and against whom hast thou exalted thy voice, and lifted up thine eyes on high? even against the Holy One of Israel.

By thy messengers thou hast reproached the Lord, and hast said, With the multitude of my chariots I am come up to the height of the mountains, to the sides of Lebanon, and will cut down the tall cedar trees thereof, and the choice fir trees thereof: and I will enter into the lodgings of his borders, and into the forest of his Carmel.

I have digged and drunk strange waters, and with the sole of my feet have I dried up all the rivers of besieged places.

Hast thou not heard long ago how I have done it, and of ancient times that I have formed it? now have I brought it to pass, that thou shouldest be to lay waste fenced cities into ruinous heaps.

Therefore their inhabitants were of small power, they were dismayed and confounded; they were as the grass of the field, and as the green herb, as the grass on the housetops, and as corn blasted before it be grown up.

But I know thy abode, and thy going out, and thy coming in, and thy rage against me.

Because thy rage against me and thy tumult is come up into mine ears, therefore I will put my hook in thy nose, and my bridle in thy lips, and I will turn thee back by the way by which thou camest.

And this shall be a sign unto thee, Ye shall eat this year such things as grow of themselves, and in the second year that which springeth of the same; and in the third year sow ye, and reap, and plant vineyards, and eat the fruits thereof.

And the remnant that is escaped of the house of Judah shall yet again take root downward, and bear fruit upward.

For out of Jerusalem shall go forth a remnant, and they that escape out of mount Zion: the zeal of the Lord of hosts shall do this.

Therefore thus saith the Lord concerning the king of Assyria, He shall not come into this city, nor shoot an arrow there, nor come before it with shield, nor cast a bank against it.

By the way that he came, by the same shall he return, and shall not come into this city, saith the Lord.

For I will defend this city, to save it, for mine own sake, and for my servant David's sake.

AND IT CAME TO PASS THAT NIGHT, THAT THE ANGEL OF THE LORD WENT OUT, AND SMOTE IN THE CAMP OF THE ASSYRIANS AN HUNDRED FOURSCORE AND FIVE THOUSAND: AND WHEN THEY AROSE EARLY IN THE MORNING, BEHOLD, THEY WERE ALL DEAD CORPSES.

2 Kings 19:1-35

13. PRAYER SECURES ANGELIC INTERVENTION FOR THE PSALMIST.

Plead my cause O Lord! Fight against those who fight against me! Angel activity increases around you as you pray. Your enemy is chased away by angels that are released around you. The way of your enemy will be dark and slippery because of the angels that have come into the picture.

PLEAD MY CAUSE, O LORD, WITH THEM THAT STRIVE WITH ME: fight against them that fight against me. Take hold of shield and buckler, and stand up for mine help. Draw out also the spear, and stop the way against them that persecute me: say unto my soul, I am thy salvation. Let them be confounded and put to shame that seek after my soul: let them be turned back and brought to confusion that devise my hurt. Let them be as chaff before the wind: and LET THE ANGEL OF THE LORD CHASE

THEM. LET THEIR WAY BE DARK AND SLIPPERY: AND LET THE ANGEL OF THE LORD PERSECUTE THEM.

Psalm 35:1-6

14. PRAYER SECURES ANGELIC INTERVENTION FOR DAVID.

There is increased angel activity because you call on the lord and trust in him. As you call upon the Lord, God will give his trusted angels a commission to look after you. It is important that you call upon the Lord. Prayer secures angelic participation in your life.

There shall no evil befall thee, neither shall any plague come nigh thy dwelling. FOR HE SHALL GIVE HIS ANGELS CHARGE OVER THEE, TO KEEP THEE IN ALL THY WAYS. They shall bear thee up in their hands, lest thou dash thy foot against a stone. Thou shalt tread upon the lion and adder: the young lion and the dragon shalt thou trample under feet. Because he hath set his love upon me, therefore will I deliver him: I will set him on high, because he hath known my name. HE SHALL CALL UPON ME, AND I WILL ANSWER HIM: I will be with him in trouble; I will deliver him, and honour him. With long life will I satisfy him, and shew him my salvation.

Psalm 91:10-16

15. PRAYER SECURED ANGELIC INTERVENTION FOR DANIEL IN THE LION'S DEN.

Angel activity was greatly increased around Daniel as he prayed three times a day. Daniel went to prison because he prayed three times a day. Praying three times a day caused angels to be released in Daniel's life. These angels, who were activated by Daniel's prayer, protected Daniel from the lions. You can rest assured that your regular prayers are causing the release of angels.

Now when Daniel knew that the writing was signed, he went into his house; and his windows being open in his chamber toward Jerusalem, HE KNEELED UPON HIS KNEES THREE TIMES A DAY, AND PRAYED, AND GAVE THANKS BEFORE HIS GOD, AS HE DID AFORETIME.

Daniel 6:10

Then said Daniel unto the king, O king, live for ever.

MY GOD HATH SENT HIS ANGEL, AND HATH SHUT THE LIONS' MOUTHS, THAT THEY HAVE NOT HURT ME: FORASMUCH AS BEFORE HIM INNOCENCY WAS FOUND IN ME; AND ALSO BEFORE THEE, O KING, HAVE I DONE NO HURT.

Then was the king exceeding glad for him, and commanded that they should take Daniel up out of the den. So Daniel was taken up out of the den, and no manner of hurt was found upon him, because he believed in his God.

And the king commanded, and they brought those men which had accused Daniel, and they cast them into the den of lions, them, their children, and their wives; and the lions had the mastery of them, and brake all their bones in pieces or ever they came at the bottom of the den.

Daniel 6:21-24

16. PRAYER SECURED ANGELIC INTERVENTION FOR DANIEL.

In this famous vision, a mighty angel was sent to Daniel. This angel's loins were girded with fine gold, his body was like beryl, his face was like lightning and his eyes were like lamps of fire. Angel activity increased in Daniel's life as he sought the lord and prayed for his nation. Three weeks of prayer yielded a mighty angelic intervention. The angel admitted that he had been sent because of Daniel's prayers. I am come because of thy words" is what the angel said. Angels come to places because of the words and prayers of God's servants.

In the third year of Cyrus king of Persia a thing was revealed unto Daniel, whose name was called Belteshazzar; and the thing was true, but the time appointed was long: and he understood the thing, and had understanding of the vision.

IN THOSE DAYS I DANIEL WAS MOURNING THREE FULL WEEKS.

I ATE NO PLEASANT BREAD, NEITHER CAME FLESH NOR WINE IN MY MOUTH, NEITHER DID I ANOINT MYSELF AT ALL, TILL THREE WHOLE WEEKS WERE FULFILLED.

AND IN THE FOUR AND TWENTIETH DAY OF THE FIRST MONTH, AS I WAS BY THE SIDE OF THE GREAT RIVER, WHICH IS HIDDEKEL;

THEN I LIFTED UP MINE EYES, AND LOOKED, AND BEHOLD A CERTAIN MAN CLOTHED IN LINEN, WHOSE LOINS WERE GIRDED WITH FINE GOLD OF UPHAZ:

HIS BODY ALSO WAS LIKE THE BERYL, AND HIS FACE AS THE APPEARANCE OF LIGHTNING, AND HIS EYES AS LAMPS OF FIRE, and his arms and his feet like in colour to polished brass, and the voice of his words like the voice of a multitude.

And I Daniel alone saw the vision: for the men that were with me saw not the vision; but a great quaking fell upon them, so that they fled to hide themselves.

Therefore I was left alone, and saw this great vision, and there remained no strength in me: for my comeliness was turned in me into corruption, and I retained no strength.

Yet heard I the voice of his words: and when I heard the voice of his words, then was I in a deep sleep on my face, and my face toward the ground.

And, behold, an hand touched me, which set me upon my knees and upon the palms of my hands.

And he said unto me, O Daniel, a man greatly beloved, understand the words that I speak unto thee, and stand upright: for unto thee am I now sent. And when he had spoken this word unto me, I stood trembling. Then said he unto me, Fear not, Daniel: for from the first day that thou didst set thine heart to understand, and to chasten thyself before thy God, thy words were heard, AND I AM COME FOR THY WORDS.

But the prince of the kingdom of Persia withstood me one and twenty days: but, lo, Michael, one of the chief princes, came to help me; and I remained there with the kings of Persia.

Now I am come to make thee understand what shall befall thy people in the latter days: for yet the vision is for many days.

And when he had spoken such words unto me, I set my face toward the ground, and I became dumb.

Daniel 10:1-15

17. PRAYER SECURED ANGELIC INTERVENTION FOR JESUS IN GETHSEMANE.

Angels multiplied around Jesus as he prayed in the garden of Gethsemane. As Jesus prayed, angels were drawn to the Garden of Gethsemane. You may be in a garden or in the bedroom. Angels will come to the location when you pray. Whether you are on a mountain or in a valley you can expect angels to flock there just because they hear the sound of prayer. Angels love prayer. Angels are drawn to prayer. Angels will come to the room you are praying in.

And when he was at the place, he said unto them, pray that ye enter not into temptation. AND HE WAS WITHDRAWN FROM THEM ABOUT A STONE'S CAST, AND KNEELED DOWN, AND PRAYED, SAYING, FATHER, IF THOU BE WILLING, REMOVE THIS CUP FROM ME: NEVERTHELESS NOT MY WILL, BUT THINE, BE DONE. AND THERE APPEARED AN ANGEL UNTO HIM FROM HEAVEN, STRENGTHENING

HIM. And being in an agony he prayed more earnestly: and his sweat was as it were great drops of blood falling down to the ground.

Luke 22:40-44

18. PRAYER SECURES ANGELIC INTERVENTION FOR JESUS IN THE WILDERNESS.

Angels multiplied around Jesus as he prayed in the wilderness. When you go to the wilderness to pray, do not think you are alone. Angels will follow you to the most lonely and deserted spot. You can never be truly alone when you are praying. Angels are somewhere in the vicinity. As Jesus waited on God in the wilderness, angels flocked there. Angels love the prayer atmosphere. They love people who pray. They love coming for prayer meetings. Angels even come for private prayer meetings. Jesus was having a private prayer meeting but angels still came there.

AND HE WAS THERE IN THE WILDERNESS FORTY DAYS, tempted of Satan; and was with the wild beasts; AND THE ANGELS MINISTERED UNTO HIM. Now after that John was put in prison, Jesus came into Galilee, preaching the gospel of the kingdom of God,

Mark 1:13-14

CHAPTER 7

Pray for Forgiveness

When Jesus saw their faith, he said unto the sick of the palsy, SON, THY SINS BE FORGIVEN THEE. I SAY UNTO THEE, ARISE, AND TAKE UP THY BED, AND GO THY WAY INTO THINE HOUSE. And immediately he arose, took up the bed, and went forth before them all; insomuch that they were all amazed, and glorified God, saying, We never saw it on this fashion.

Mark 2:5, 11-12

In the passage above, this man, sick of the palsy, received forgiveness from Jesus. He did not even receive a prayer from Jesus. Jesus did not even lay hands on him. All he received was forgiveness of sins! God forgave him for his sins. The fact that God sent Jesus into the world so that men would receive forgiveness of sins reveals the importance of forgiveness of sins.

Forgiveness of sins is one of the greatest blessings one can ever receive. This forgiveness that he received led to many great blessings in this man's life. He received healing, deliverance and liberty. The testimony of the man sick of the palsy, who was forgiven reveals for all time the powerful effects of forgiveness.

Ten Powerful Effects of Forgiveness

1. Forgiveness of the man sick of the palsy led to his healing.

2. Forgiveness of the man sick of the palsy led to the removal of what was killing him.

3. Forgiveness of the man sick of the palsy ended suffering.

4. Forgiveness of the man sick of the palsy brought him liberty from the stretcher.

5. Forgiveness of the man sick of the palsy took away the curse in his life.

6. Forgiveness of the man sick of the palsy enabled him to get a job. His sickness

   prevented him from being employed.

7. Forgiveness of the man sick of the palsy brought him a brand new life.

8. Forgiveness of the man sick of the palsy ended his sadness and depression.

9. Forgiveness of the man sick of the palsy ended the isolation that he felt because of his paralysis.

10. Forgiveness of the man sick of the palsy enabled this man to get married.

Marriage and relationships are greatly healed and blessed through forgiveness.

Why You Need to Pray for Forgiveness

1. Pray for forgiveness because you are a sinner.

As it is written, There is none righteous, no, not one:

Romans 3:10

Praying for forgiveness of sins is important because we are dreadful sinners who come before a righteous God pleading for good things to be done to us. You may be the school prefect and you may have won many awards and prizes. This does not change the fact that you are a terrible sinner. You may be a pastor. You may be anointed. You may be a Reverend Minister or a Bishop. But you are still a sinner. That is why you need to confess your sins. There is none righteous! Not even one person! This is not a cliché. This is not false humility. This is truth! There is none righteous, not even one person.

2. Pray for forgiveness because you have inherited sins.

Wherefore, as by one man sin entered into the world, and death by sin; and so death passed upon all men, for that all have sinned:

Romans 5:12

Everyone has inherited sin from their fathers, grandfathers and sister. The presence of inherited sins is the reason for death and judgment amongst the most seemingly righteous people. You may not commit any particular hideous sin that you are aware of but the sins you have inherited from your parents, grandparents and ancestors are having an effect. Sin has entered into the world

67

and death has followed suit. Notice what the scripture says: death has passed upon all men. Death is something that moves and occupies its rightful place. Death has a right to appear in our lives because we have inherited sins from our parents, grandparents and ancestors.

3.   Pray for forgiveness because God saw everything you did.

The eyes of the Lord are in every place, beholding the evil and the good.

Proverbs 15:3

When we pray, we really need God to ignore our past sins. The reason is that if our past sins, mistakes and crimes are brought up as we are pleading before the Lord, we will become obnoxious to God. Our sins are rottenness and corruption before the Lord. We have practiced every sin before God and he has seen everything we have ever done or said.   God sees into every corner and into every sin and failing of our lives. Nothing is hid before Him.

4.   Pray for forgiveness because your heart is bare before God.

Neither is there any creature that is not manifest in his sight: but all things are naked and opened unto the eyes of him with whom we have to do.

Hebrews 4:13

As we stand before the throne of God, He cannot be deceived by our good words and good presentation. Many people go to court and put up a good presentation with good words and good arguments. With a good presentation and good arguments, many deceivers and wicked people escape their rightful judgment. This is not so with God. Everything is bare and manifest and naked before Him. Your heart, your soul and your feelings are bare before the Lord.

It is important to confess your sins regularly. At every opportunity where you come into the presence of the Lord, you must confess your sins. Confess your sins in the evening; during the day you will have several opportunities to sin, to be angry and to say something wrong. Confess your sins in the morning; during the night you may commit sins and you may even have bad dreams that pollute your soul.

CHAPTER 8

Four Prayers of Confession

I acknowledged my sin unto thee, and mine iniquity
have I not hid. I said, I will confess my transgressions
unto the LORD; and thou forgavest the iniquity of my
sin. Selah.

Psalms 32:5

If we confess our sins, he is faithful and just to forgive
us our sins, and to cleanse us from all unrighteousness.

1 John 1:9

1.   **Confess your sins before the Lord.**

For if ye forgive men their trespasses, your heavenly Father will also forgive you:

Matthew 6:14

It is important to confess all the sins that you have committed. Do not be afraid to keep confessing the same things. Most of us confess the same things several times over. Unfortunately, our human flesh causes us to bend over in the same wrong direction many times. As you confess your sin to the Lord, you are displaying honesty and you are being real.

God can see through you, anyway. You cannot hide or act phony before God. You must be real when you go before His presence. Confess your sins right at the beginning of your prayer time. Confess your sins at any time during your prayer time. Confess your sins just after you have sinned. Never stop confessing your sins.

2.   **Confess your transgressions before the Lord.**

Seventy weeks are determined upon thy people and upon thy holy city, to finish the TRANSGRESSION, and to make an end OF SINS, and to make reconciliation for INIQUITY, and to bring in everlasting righteousness, and to seal up the vision and prophecy, and to anoint the most Holy.

Daniel 9:24

All three types of sins are mentioned in the verse above. The three types of sins are ordinary sins or trespasses, transgressions and iniquities.

A transgression is a type of sin in which you break away from the usual. The word "transgression" is translated from the Hebrew word "Pesha". It means "expansion, breaking away, crossing certain boundaries".

71

When you commit a "pesha" (transgression), you cross a certain boundary. For instance, within sexual sins, there are certain boundaries and limits that people keep. When you cross a boundary, you have committed a transgression.

There are many ways in which we cross boundaries in sin.

You can cross a boundary when you actively tell lies and speak untruths. When you become a liar, you have crossed into a demonic dimension of your sin.

When you criticize and dishonor the Lord's anointed, you have sinned and joined murmurers and disloyal people in the church.

The crossing of boundaries has far-reaching effects. When the church allows the killing of newborn babies as a form of abortion, it has also crossed a boundary.

When human beings campaign to marry animals, we have crossed a certain boundary.

When we cross from accepting fornication to accepting sexual perversions, we have committed a transgression because we have crossed a certain boundary of sinful life. When the church allows sexual perversions to be practiced by priests, it has crossed even more boundaries and expanded the scope of accepted sinful practice.

When they criticized Moses, a prophet who saw God face to face, they crossed a boundary. It was this boundary that Miriam crossed and contracted leprosy.

My servant Moses is not so, who is faithful in all mine house. With him will I speak mouth to mouth, even apparently, and not in dark speeches; and the similitude of the LORD shall he behold: wherefore then were ye not afraid to speak against my servant Moses? And the anger of the LORD was kindled against them; and he departed. And the cloud departed from off the tabernacle; and, behold,

Miriam became leprous, white as snow: and Aaron looked upon Miriam, and, behold, she was leprous.

Numbers 12:7-10

3.   Confess your iniquities before the Lord.

Seventy weeks are determined upon thy people and upon thy holy city, to finish the TRANSGRESSION, and to make an end OF SINS, and to make reconciliation for INIQUITY, and to bring in everlasting righteousness, and to seal up the vision and prophecy, and to anoint the most Holy.

Daniel 9:24

It is important to also confess your iniquities. Iniquity comes from the word "avon avon". Iniquity means perversity. It speaks of something that is twisted, bowed down and crooked.

Your iniquity is your usual path or the usual sin that you have grown to commit regularly and effortlessly.

It may be the sin of criticism. Criticism can become an iniquity because it is what you commit habitually, repeatedly and naturally. There are some people who will criticize you as smoothly as they breathe. Their next remark will be a sarcastic, cutting and sneering comment.

There are those who criticize the people they love because it is an iniquity that is a part of them. It is a twistedness that they have grown up with. It is a perversion that they have learned to live with. To be without criticism would be abnormal in their lives. They always have someone they criticize. I once met someone who had an iniquity of criticism and sarcastic speech. I found out who were the ones in her life who received the most criticism and she answered, "My closest sister and friend is the one I criticize most." How can you criticize your closest sister and friend even more than your enemies? It is obvious that this Christian had developed an unfortunate perversion and twistedness of her character which caused her to criticize even people that she loved.

Some people have sexual iniquities. They will commit sexual sin with anyone they encounter. To commit a sexual sin would be as easy as drinking a glass of water. Fornication and adultery happen easily, smoothly, frequently and repeatedly when a person suffers from the iniquity of sexual sin.

There are those who tell lies as though they are breathing. Breathing is effortless, frequent and continuous. These are the people who grow up and become actors, deceiving everyone around them. Deception is second nature. When lying and deception are iniquities in your life, acting and hypocrisy are easy and natural. Hypocrites can be employed in Hollywood because they act out their lies from morning to evening. It would not occur to anyone that they are very different from what they present themselves to be.

Many of the actors in Hollywood are not strong men who can fight or even shoot guns. Yet we see some of them as super heroes who are able to fight with a hundred men at a time.

Do not allow the perversion of hypocrisy to develop in your life. Deception must not be your constant, repeated sin!

Do not allow a sin to develop into a perversion and a twisted lifestyle. If you have iniquities, it is important to confess and forsake them.

4.   Confess your debts before God.

And forgive us our debts, as we forgive our debtors.
Matthew 6:12

Your debts are your obligations. Your debts are things you owe God. Confession of your debts is what some people call confessing the sins of omission. A debt is something you owe! A debt is an obligation you were expected to fulfill.

Throughout the Bible, we realize that sins of omission are seen as terrible sins. In the parable Jesus gave us, one person was given five talents and another was given two talents. The last person was given one talent. The person with one talent did nothing. Yet Jesus said to him, "You are an evil person. You are a wicked and slothful man." Why did Jesus give such a scathing denunciation of this servant?

> Then he which had received the one talent came and said, Lord, I knew thee that thou art an hard man, reaping where thou hast not sown, and gathering where thou hast not strawed: And I was afraid, and went and hid thy talent in the earth: lo, there thou hast that is thine. His lord answered and said unto him, Thou wicked and slothful servant, thou knewest that I reap where I sowed not, and gather where I have not strawed: Thou oughtest therefore to have put my money to the exchangers, and then at my coming I should have received mine own with usury. Take therefore the talent from him, and give it unto him which hath ten talents.

> Matthew 25:24-28

How come "doing nothing" is described as wickedness? God considers "doing nothing" to be sinful. He expects you to be up and about, accomplishing, performing and doing all that He has asked you to do. Today, there are many nations that debate whether omitting to do something is a crime or not. Everyone has a different opinion.

If there is a bystander who sees someone in need and does not exert necessary effort to help, has he committed a crime or not? In some countries, standing by and "doing nothing" is not a crime. To them, a crime is said to have been committed when you have *done something*. When you have *done nothing,* no crime is said to have been committed.

I want you to notice that in the Common Law of England, no crime is said to have occurred for failing to act in the event of another person being in danger.

However, according to the Dutch Criminal Law, he who being a witness to the instantaneous mortal danger of another and fails to provide such help and the death of a person does happen, the person will be punished with imprisonment up to three months for not helping.

In Finland, the sin of omission is also taken seriously in Section 15 of their criminal code. It states that a person who knows that another is in mortal or serious danger to his or her health, and does not give or procure such assistance that in view of his or her options and the nature of the situation can reasonably be expected, shall be sentenced for neglect of rescue to a fine or to imprisonment for, at most, six months.

In Israel, the law requires anyone to assist a person in danger or, at the very least, call for help. People who help in good faith are not liable for damages. Helpers are eligible for compensation for damage caused to them during their assistance.

What is Jesus' Law?

According to Jesus it is wickedness to stand by and do nothing! It is wrong to stand by as people go to hell and fail to preach to them and tell them about Jesus. It is wrong to be silent when you can speak. It is wickedness to do nothing when you can do something. You will not be judged by Finnish Law, Dutch Law or British Law. You will be judged by Jesus' law.

For the Father judgeth no man, but hath committed all judgment unto the Son:

John 5:22

CHAPTER 9

The Blessing of Confession of Sins

> **Confess your faults one to another, and pray one for another, that ye may be healed. The effectual fervent prayer of a righteous man availeth much.**
>
> **James 5:16**

There are many blessings for confessing your sins. The presence of sin leads to many evils in your life. The way to get rid of sins is to confess them. Let us go through the scriptures and see the blessings that come when you confess your sins.

1. Confession of sins brings God's hand into your situation.

Behold, the LORD'S hand is not shortened, that it cannot save; neither his ear heavy, that it cannot hear: But your iniquities have separated between you and your God, and your sins have hid his face from you, that he will not hear.

Isaiah 59:1-2

It will always seem as though God's hand is short when you do not confess your sins. It will seem as though God cannot and does not want to get involved deeply in your issues. That is not the case. God's hand is right there to help you. He is capable! Your sins have put God out of reach. Sins separate you from God in such a way that God seems far away.

2. Confession of sin leads to healing.

Confess your faults one to another, and pray one for another, that ye may be healed. The effectual fervent prayer of a righteous man availeth much.

James 5:16

You will notice how many people received their healing when their sins were addressed. Sin is a precursor to death. Sickness is the major agent through which death comes into our lives. Therefore, sin is always connected to sickness. It is important to confess your sins, lest many diseases come upon you.

You will notice that there are diseases that children are born with. Some of us have inherited illnesses. Even before you committed your first sin, you may have been afflicted by sickness and disease. Why is this? We are afflicted by sins and diseases because we have equally inherited sins from our fathers, grandfathers and ancestors. Let me give you four examples of how healing and deliverance from sickness is directly connected to sins being forgiven.

a. **Healing of the paralytic through forgiveness:** The man carried by four people was forgiven his sins and it resulted in his healing.

> And, behold, men brought in a bed a man which was taken with a palsy: and they sought means to bring him in, and to lay him before him. And when they could not find by what way they might bring him in because of the multitude, they went upon the housetop, and let him down through the tiling with his couch into the midst before Jesus. And when he saw their faith, he said unto him, Man, thy sins are forgiven thee....
>
> Whether is easier, to say, Thy sins be forgiven thee; or to say, Rise up and walk? But that ye may know that the Son of man hath power upon earth to forgive sins, (he said unto the sick of the palsy,) I say unto thee, Arise, and take up thy couch, and go into thine house.

Luke 5:18-20, 23-24

b. **Healing of blind Bartimaeus through forgiveness:** Blind Bartimaeus prayed for nothing other than mercy. Blind Bartimaeus cried, "Lord have mercy on me." The mercy that blind Bartimaeus received was the healing of his eyes.

> And they came to Jericho: and as he went out of Jericho with his disciples and a great number of people, blind Bartimaeus, the son of Timaeus, sat by the highway side begging. And when he heard that it was Jesus of Nazareth, he began to cry out, and say, JESUS, THOU SON OF DAVID, HAVE MERCY ON ME. And many charged him that he should hold his peace: but he cried the more a great deal, Thou Son of David, have mercy on me...
>
> And Jesus answered and said unto him, what wilt thou that I should do unto thee? The blind man said unto him, Lord, that I might receive my sight. And Jesus said unto him, Go

thy way; thy faith hath made thee whole. And immediately he received his sight, and followed Jesus in the way.

Mark 10:46-48, 51-52

c. **Healing of the blind man through forgiveness:** The blind man in the ninth chapter of John received his healing from Jesus. Jesus was asked an important question, "Who sinned that this man was born blind?" Jesus knew that sin would lead to sickness. The disciples of Jesus knew that sicknesses came from sin. The terrible disease of blindness had descended on this man and they knew that it must have been caused by a sin.

And as Jesus passed by, he saw a man which was blind from his birth. And his disciples asked him, saying, Master, who did sin, this man, or his parents, that he was born blind? Jesus answered, neither hath this man sinned, nor his parents: but that the works of God should be made manifest in him. I must work the works of him that sent me, while it is day: the night cometh, when no man can work. As long as I am in the world, I am the light of the world. When he had thus spoken, he spat on the ground, and made clay of the spittle, and he anointed the eyes of the blind man with the clay, And said unto him, Go, wash in the pool of Siloam, (which is by interpretation, Sent.) He went his way therefore, and washed, and came seeing.

John 9:1-7

3. Confession of sins leads to prosperity.

He that covereth his sins shall not prosper: but whoso confesseth and forsaketh them shall have mercy.

Proverbs 28:13

Prosperity will be far away from you when you do not confess your sins. Your sins literally steal your prosperity. Do you want to prosper? It is important that you do not stand before God and act as though your sins are covered. All things are bare and naked before Him. Do not think that only sowing seeds and giving offerings will lead to prosperity. You may sow all the seeds you have and give all the tithes and offerings you can, but if you live in sin you will not prosper.

Prosperity does not only come from hard work. Prosperity comes from confession of sins! You may be talented and very hardworking. But if you live in sin and practice sin, you will lose the prosperity that you should have had from your hard work.

Many hardworking and talented men have lost the money they earned through gambling, fornication, adultery, alcoholism, drugs and the like. Their sins robbed them of their prosperity. It is important to confess and to forsake your sin so that you can allow the prosperity that you are due to flow into your life. May you never be robbed of prosperity because of your sins that you did not confess!

4. Confession of sin causes the presence of the Holy Spirit to return to you.

Create in me a clean heart, O God; and renew a right spirit within me. Cast me not away from thy presence; and take not thy holy spirit from me. Restore unto me the joy of thy salvation; and uphold me with thy free spirit.

Psalms 51:10-12

David sinned greatly against the Lord. He knew that he was about to lose the presence of the Holy Spirit. When you commit a crime against your friend you will lose his presence. You will lose the friendship that you once enjoyed. Sin causes separation from the presence of the Holy Spirit. When you confess your sin, you open yourself up to the presence of the Holy Spirit.

5. Confession of sins causes a restoration of your joy.

Restore unto me the joy of thy salvation; and uphold me with thy free spirit.

Psalms 51:12

Depression is a side effect of sin. Sinners are sad people. Sin makes you sad. Sin makes you lose your joy, your cheerfulness and your happiness. You may think that people are excited when they sin. Most people are sad after they have finished committing a sin. Confess your sin to God and He will restore the joy of your salvation.

6. Confession of sin brings an end to the curse.

The ninth chapter of Daniel shows the long prayers of Daniel that resulted in a significant vision.

Daniel's prayers consisted mainly of confession of his sins and the sins of his nation, Israel. There is an important revelation about curses that you will see in Daniel's prayers. In this prayer, Daniel revealed that curses are poured out because of sins. Do you want a curse to be poured out on you?

Yea, all Israel have transgressed thy law, even by departing, that they might not obey thy voice; THEREFORE THE CURSE IS POURED UPON US, and the oath that is written in the law of Moses the servant of God, because we have sinned against him.

Daniel 9:11

Daniel prayed fervently to the Lord so that the curse, which had been poured out, would be averted or neutralized.

Prayers can neutralize curses. But specifically, confession of sins can neutralize a curse in your life. You must notice how Daniel was speaking, praying and confessing his sins when the angel appeared.

The appearance of this angel signified some relief from the curse that was upon Israel. The appearance of the angel was a visit from heaven. Any visit from heaven will help to neutralize and alleviate the curse that is on your life. You will receive a visitation from heaven as you spend time praying and confessing your sins.

And whiles I was speaking, and praying, and confessing my sin and the sin of my people Israel, and presenting my supplication before the Lord my God for the holy mountain of my God; Yea, whiles I was speaking in prayer, even the man Gabriel, whom I had seen in the vision at the beginning, being caused to fly swiftly, touched me about the time of the evening oblation.

Daniel 9:20-21

7. Confession of sins causes a restoration of your life.

Brethren, if a man be overtaken in a fault, ye which are spiritual, RESTORE such an one in the spirit of meekness; considering thyself, lest thou also be tempted.

Galatians 6:1

Sin causes various problems in our lives. Sin causes you to need restoration. In the twenty-third psalm, the Psalmist says, "He restoreth my soul." Restoration and healing will come to your life through confession of sin. If we confess our sins He is faithful and just to forgive us. God is a God of restoration.

Restoration involves making you as though you never committed any of those sins. Why would God have to restore you if you were not destroyed?

Restoration involves building up the old and wasted places. Why would God need to build the old wastes if you had not become a wasted swamp in the house of God?

And they shall build the old wastes, they shall raise up the former desolations, and they shall repair the waste cities, the desolations of many generations.

Isaiah 61:4

Restoration involves healing you of the sicknesses that have come to you from your sins.

83

Restoration would involve stabilizing your life. Why would God need to stabilize you if you were not destabilized and unsettled by your sin?

But the God of all grace, who hath called us unto his eternal glory by Christ Jesus, after that ye have suffered a while, make you perfect, stablish, strengthen, settle you.

1 Peter 5:10

Restoration would involve making you clean again. Why would God need to sanctify you if you were not polluted and corrupted?

All these restoration blessings will come to you when you confess your sins. Confession eradicates sins and brings about restoration. God is a God of restoration, sanctification and redemption! God is a rebuilder of the old wastes!

CHAPTER 10

Pray to a Father!

Pray to a Friend!

Pray to a Judge!

And he spake a parable unto them to this end, that men ought always to pray, and not to faint; Saying, There was in a city a judge, which feared not God, neither regarded man: And there was a widow in that city; and she came unto him, saying, Avenge me of mine adversary. And he would not for a while: but afterward he said within himself, Though I fear not God, nor regard man; Yet because this widow troubleth me, I will avenge her, lest by her continual coming she weary me. AND THE LORD SAID, HEAR WHAT THE UNJUST JUDGE SAITH. AND SHALL NOT GOD AVENGE HIS OWN ELECT, WHICH CRY DAY AND NIGHT UNTO HIM, THOUGH HE BEAR LONG WITH THEM? I tell you that he will avenge them speedily. Nevertheless when the Son of man cometh, shall he find faith on the earth?

Luke 18:1-8

J esus taught us to maintain three relationships and attitudes when we pray. We must maintain the attitude of talking to a father when we pray. We must maintain the attitude of talking to a judge when we are pray. Finally, we must maintain the posture of talking to a friend when we pray. All these three different stances make a difference when we pray. Let us look at the three postures and see what the differences are. Father, friend, judge!

1. PRAYING TO A FATHER:

AFTER THIS MANNER THEREFORE PRAY YE: OUR FATHER which art in heaven, Hallowed be thy name. Thy kingdom come. Thy will be done in earth, as it is in heaven. Give us this day our daily bread. And forgive us our debts, as we forgive our debtors. And lead us not into temptation, but deliver us from evil: For thine is the kingdom, and the power, and the glory, for ever. Amen.

Matthew 6:9-13

Praying to God as a father is to come before someone whom you are sure loves you. God loves you and He truly loves you as a father. God pities us as a father pities his children.

Like as a father pitieth his children, so the LORD pitieth them that fear him.

Psalms 103:13

You can pray to the Father about His will. The will of the father is what prevails in the house. It is what the father desires and likes that is eaten in the house. If the father wishes to have parties and banquets, there will be parties and banquets in the house. If the father desires to play golf, golf will be important in that home. I once saw a famous golfer playing golf with his son. Golf was important in that home because it was important to the famous father of that house.

If church is important to the father, people in the house will go to church and know about God. Whenever you are praying to the Father, you have to be conscious of the will of the Father. It is the father's will that is performed in a home. That is why we pray, "Thy will be done in earth as it is in heaven". It is because we are praying to a father.

You can pray to the Father about your daily bread. It is the father who provides daily bread for the home. Anytime you call on God as a father, your daily bread will be guaranteed.

Mistakes are forgiven by fathers. Friends may not forgive you. Colleagues may not forgive you. Pastors may not forgive you. But fathers will forgive you! It is to a father that you can look for pity and forgiveness. You have many obligations to your father. You have many debts that you owe your father for all that he has done for you. He brought you up. He cared for you. He gave you his genes. He gave you his possessions. He gave you a name. He provided for you. You are always in debt to your father. This is why we pray the prayer, "Forgive us our debts" to our Father.

Your father is also the one who can deliver you from evil and lead you away from temptation.

Through the direction, instructions, teachings and wisdom of a father, you will be led away from temptation and delivered from evil. This is why you pray to the Father to lead you away from temptation and deliver you from evil.

2.   PRAYING TO A FRIEND:

And he said unto them, WHICH OF YOU SHALL HAVE A FRIEND, and shall go unto him at midnight, and say unto him, Friend, lend me three loaves; for a friend of mine in his journey is come to me, and I have nothing to set before him? And he from within shall answer and say, Trouble me not: the door is now shut, and my children are with me in bed; I cannot rise and

give thee. I say unto you, Though he will not rise and give him, because he is his friend, yet because of his importunity he will rise and give him as many as he needeth.

Luke 11:5-8

When you have he attitude of speaking to a friend in prayer, you can ask God for your small things and your embarrassing things. In the scripture above, Jesus depicts the Father as a friend to whom you can come and ask for things that you need.

To a friend, nothing is too trivial or insignificant. Asking for bread at midnight is not an embarrassment because he is a friend. Friends are people that you ask minor and trivial things. When you take the posture of speaking to a friend in prayer, you can ask God for your small things, and your embarrassing things. When you are talking to a friend, you never think that you are disturbing or troubling him.

When you are praying as a friend, you can speak to God about the awkward things in your life. You can discuss the distressing and humiliating things that you just cannot talk about. When you are praying to God as a friend, you can speak to Him about anyone that annoys you. When you are praying as a friend, you can speak to God about your financial needs, your marital needs, your social needs, your relationship needs and your spiritual needs.

When you are praying to God as a friend you can speak to Him about personal things. When you are praying to God as a friend you can speak to Him about intimate things. When you are praying as a friend, you can speak to God about anything that disturbs you or makes you unhappy.

When you are praying to God as a friend you can speak to Him about your secrets. Friends always share secrets.

When you are praying to God as a friend you can speak to Him about the petty issues of your life.

When you are praying to God as a friend you can speak to Him about any difficulty you have in your relationships or in your marriage.

3. PRAYING TO A JUDGE:

And he spake a parable unto them to this end, that men ought always to pray, and not to faint; Saying, There was in a city a judge, which feared not God, neither regarded man: And there was a widow in that city; and she came unto him, saying, Avenge me of mine adversary. And he would not for a while: but afterward he said within himself, Though I fear not God, nor regard man; Yet because this widow troubleth me, I will avenge her, lest by her continual coming she weary me. AND THE LORD SAID, HEAR WHAT THE UNJUST JUDGE SAITH. AND SHALL NOT GOD AVENGE HIS OWN ELECT, WHICH CRY DAY AND NIGHT UNTO HIM, THOUGH HE BEAR LONG WITH THEM? I tell you that he will avenge them speedily. Nevertheless when the Son of man cometh, shall he find faith on the earth?

Luke 18:1-8

In this story, Jesus compares the Father to a judge. A judge is someone who has to take a decision that will change the lives of everyone. By a judge's decision, you can have your sleeping place changed. By a judge's decision, you can have victory over an enemy that is tormenting you.

By a judge's decision, wicked people and wickedness will be put down, silenced and flattened. God is a judge! He puts down one and sets up another. When you come to God in prayer you must also see Him as a judge. Through your prayers to God as a judge, God will put someone down and set up another.

Pray to God and call on him as a judge. God will intervene and pour His judgment on people who have mistreated you and mishandled you.

BUT GOD IS THE JUDGE: he putteth down one, and setteth up another. For in the hand of the Lord there is a cup, and the wine is red; it is full of mixture; and he poureth out of the same: but the dregs thereof, all the wicked of the earth shall wring them out, and drink them. But I will declare for ever; I will sing praises to the God of Jacob. All the horns of the wicked also will I cut off; but the horns of the righteous shall be exalted.

Psalm 75:7-10

Through your prayers to God as a judge, vengeance will come to you. It is important to call on God so that you experience the vengeance of God on those that torment you. Notice the prayer of the psalmist. He calls on the God to whom vengeance belongs and asks Him to show Himself.

If you do not call on the God to whom vengeance belongs, He may not show Himself as a judge. It is important not to take vengeance yourself. It is written, "Vengeance is mine, I will repay." God is the One who repays people for their wickedness. There will be no need to rise up in judgment and take up vengeance on anyone who has done you harm. God is a specialist in taking vengeance.

O LORD GOD, TO WHOM VENGEANCE BELONGETH; O GOD, TO WHOM VENGEANCE BELONGETH, SHEW THYSELF. LIFT UP THYSELF, THOU JUDGE OF THE EARTH: render a reward to the proud. Lord, how long shall the wicked, how long shall the wicked triumph? How long shall they utter and speak hard things? And all the workers of iniquity boast themselves? They break in pieces thy people, O Lord, and afflict thine heritage. They slay the widow and the stranger, and murder the fatherless. Yet they say, The Lord shall not see, neither shall the God of Jacob regard it. Understand, ye brutish among the people: and ye fools, when will ye be wise? He that planted the ear, shall he not hear? He that formed the eye, shall he not see? He that chastiseth the heathen,

shall not he correct? He that teacheth man knowledge, shall not he know? The Lord knoweth the thoughts of man, that they are vanity.

Psalm 94:1-11

Conclusion

Prayer changes things! It is my hope that this little book will help you to believe in prayer and to pray even more.

May you spend many hours in the presence of God!

May angels appear and participate in your life!

May angels intervene in your crisis! God will change many things in your life through prayer!

May you experience the truth in these words, "Prayer changes things"!

To the making of many books there is no end.

BV - #0025 - 150223 - C0 - 212/135/6 - PB - 9600690000710 - Gloss Lamination